Tech Leadership 4.0

Leading in a Technologically Driven World

By Robert Pasick, Ph.D. & Michael A. Anleitner

Copyright and Contact Information

© 2020: Robert Pasick, PhD. And
Michael A. Anleitner
All Rights Reserved

Rob Pasick may be contacted at
rob@robpasick.com

Michael Anleitner may be contacted at
m.anleitner.68@gmail.com

Cover Illustration:

Original Design by Zach Wills

Acknowledgements

Both authors would like to thank Dunrie Greiling for her outstanding work editing the manuscript as well as her editorial contributions.

Rob would like to thank his wife, Pat, for her support throughout 50+ years of our relationship.

Mike would like to thank his wife, Carol, for her many years of support for his work, and his son Ben and daughter Jocelyn for living the stories told in this book.

About the Authors

Dr. Rob Pasick is a professional coach, practicing psychologist, social entrepreneur, and an instructor at the University of Michigan in Ann Arbor. Rob is the author of nine other books, including *Balanced Leadership in Unbalanced Times, Conversations with My Old Dog, and Self-Aware: A Guide for Success in Work and Life.*

He and his wife Pat also reside in Ann Arbor.

Michael A. Anleitner is an engineering and management consultant and resides in Addison, Texas, near Dallas. He is also the author of *The Power of Deduction: Failure Modes & Effects Analysis for Design.*

Mike and his wife Carol spend summers in Northern Michigan.

Table of Contents

PREFACE 6
- *Can Engineers Be Great Leaders? 10*
- *How Did We Get to Where We Are? 12*
- *What Do We Mean by Balanced Leadership? 13*
- *Our World Needs Balanced Leadership 16*
- *The Personal Leadership Development Plan 19*
- *Understanding Balance 21*
- *That Doesn't Mean It's Easy to Stay Balanced 24*
- *Inside an Engineer's Head 25*
- *Leaving Footprints 28*

CHAPTER TWO 31
- *Establish Your Balance Points 31*
- *Ways to Ease the Way 33*
- *Teamwork Works 39*

CHAPTER THREE 43
- *Build on Your Strengths 43*
- *Discover Your Strong Points 44*
- *Draft A Personal Mission Statement 46*
- *Describe Your Vision of Success 49*
- *Define Your Core Values 52*
- *Addressing Those Other Things 55*
- *Summing Up—Your Assignment 62*

CHAPTER FOUR 64
- *Time to Get More Specific: Entering The Matrix 64*

Set Goals You Can Achieve 68
Commit to Action 71
Pick Your Support Team 72
It's Never as Easy as It Looks: Resiliency Counts .. 76
Your Goal Setting Assignment 79
A Resource for Balance: The Coach's Clipboard 80

CHAPTER FIVE 82

The Coach's Clipboard: Knowing Who You Are 82
Behavior 1. Think before you act. 82
   THE PLAYBOOK 85
Behavior 2. Recognize your blind spots and bad habits. 86
   THE PLAYBOOK 87
Behavior 3. Know your emotional IQ. 88
   THE PLAYBOOK 89
Behavior 4. Learn from your mistakes. 90
   THE PLAYBOOK 91
Behavior 5. Know your limits. 92
   THE PLAYBOOK 93
Behavior 6. Practice self-control through physical discipline. 94
   THE PLAYBOOK 95
Behavior 7. If you're stuck, get unstuck. 95
   THE PLAYBOOK 98
Behavior 8. Help yourself by helping those around you. 99
   THE PLAYBOOK 100
Behavior 9. Stop trying to control people. 100
   THE PLAYBOOK 101

Behavior 10. Apologize when you're wrong.......... **102**
   THE PLAYBOOK.. 103

Behavior 11. Lighten up. **104**
   THE PLAYBOOK.. 105

CHAPTER SIX...107

The Coach's Clipboard: Demonstrating Self-Control
.... **107**

Behavior 1. Keep tweaking your life. **107**
   THE PLAYBOOK.. 109

Behavior 2. Inspire, don't intimidate. **110**
   THE PLAYBOOK.. 114

Behavior 3. Figure out where your role begins and ends. **116**
   THE PLAYBOOK.. 117

Behavior 4. Control your temper................................ **118**
   THE PLAYBOOK.. 120

Behavior 5. Feel the fear and do it anyway. **121**
   THE PLAYBOOK.. 124

Behavior 6. Think positive. **124**
   THE PLAYBOOK.. 128

Behavior 7. Get the help you need............................ **129**
   THE PLAYBOOK.. 130

Behavior 8. Play hard.... **130**
   THE PLAYBOOK.. 132

Behavior 9. Manage your energy as well as your time. **133**
   THE PLAYBOOK.. 135

Behavior 10. Avoid cutoffs. Don't ghost anyone.... **136**
   THE PLAYBOOK.. 137

Behavior 11. Take good care of yourself. **139**
   THE PLAYBOOK.. 140

Behavior 12. Be disciplined. **142**
    THE PLAYBOOK 142

Behavior 13. Build free days into your schedule. .. **144**
    THE PLAYBOOK 145

Behavior 14. Reject the tyranny of a totally-wired world. **146**
    THE PLAYBOOK 148

CHAPTER SEVEN 149

The Coach's Clipboard: Your Enthusiasm Springs from Within… **149**

Behavior 1. Have a dream. **150**
    THE PLAYBOOK 152

Behavior 2. Commit to your dream. **153**
    THE PLAYBOOK 156

Behavior 3. Define your passion. **158**
    THE PLAYBOOK 160

Behavior 4. Accept your leadership role. **161**
    THE PLAYBOOK 164

Behavior 5. Look out of the window and into the mirror. **166**
    THE PLAYBOOK 170

Behavior 6. Don't get stuck on the dark side of human intolerance. **171**
    THE PLAYBOOK 173

CHAPTER EIGHT 175

The Coach's Clipboard: You Can Put Yourself in the Other Guy's Shoes… **175**

Behavior 1. Read the emotional cues that others transmit. **176**
    THE PLAYBOOK 178

Behavior 2. Improve your empathy skills by overcoming instinctive responses. **179**
   THE PLAYBOOK 182

Behavior 3. Fill those buckets. **183**
   THE PLAYBOOK 186

Behavior 4. Use the strengths of those around you to keep teams in balance. **188**
   THE PLAYBOOK 191

Behavior 5. Credit's like fertilizer—spread it around and watch things grow. **193**
   THE PLAYBOOK 197

Behavior 6. Help yourself by helping others. **198**
   THE PLAYBOOK 202

Behavior 7. Give to others and expect nothing in return. **204**
   THE PLAYBOOK 207

CHAPTER NINE **209**
Completing Your Personal Leadership Development Plan **209**

Sources & More Reading **215**

PREFACE

Rob and Mike first met in 2002, about one year after the 9/11 attacks in New York and Washington. Mike attended Rob's lecture on resilience at the University of Michigan's Ross School of Business as part of Michigan's annual football homecoming celebrations. The business world was just starting to recover from the disruption, and there were still major repercussions echoing around the globe. That recovery drove our initial discussion.

It was, perhaps, an omen of what was ahead. After that meeting, we kept in touch and, from time to time, collaborated on projects that involved industrial organizations. At the same time, we continued to pursue our respective consulting and teaching activities—Rob as a practicing psychologist, author, consultant, and leadership influencer, Mike as an engineering trainer and consultant working with companies around the world in manufacturing and product development. Mike taught a 3-day seminar for the Society of Automotive Engineers to prepare first time managers to balance the competing demands of technical leadership. This seminar, which was taught many times over a decade to almost 500 engineering leaders, gained top ratings from attendees and was consistently sold out.

Rob and Mike started writing this book in 2009, after yet another shock to the world: the financial collapse of 2008. Rob had just published his book *Balanced Leadership in Unbalanced Times* in early 2009 and he asked Mike to review the book.

Mike posted this review on Amazon:

> *This is a very practical and powerful book about leadership. I've been so impressed with Rob*

> Pasick's work that I have started working with him to write a sequel of sorts aimed at the technical community.
>
> This book is particularly useful at this moment in history, when so many are under such stress. Not only does the author describe sound principles for improving leadership skills, he provides 52 specific "playbook" discussions (1 per week, enough for one year) that will show you how to help yourself become a better leader.
>
> I've personally worked through many of the exercises Rob proposes, and, although I've been teaching an intensive leadership seminar for the Society of Automotive Engineering for several years, I learned a great deal doing this.

We started working on a draft, and in short order, we had something we both thought would be a great companion to Rob's original book. However, soon after, inspired by the book to make big changes in his life, Mike left his consulting business for a full-time position in the Dallas-Fort Worth area working for a large heating and air conditioning company.

Rob and Mike kept in touch, though, but we never could quite find the time, the right "fit" of ideas, or the circumstances to finish. Both of us were deeply aware that the world was changing in other ways, too. The so-called Third Wave of the Industrial Revolution was coming to an end and something new was brewing. The Third Wave started in the late 1940's and ended in the first decade of the 21st century. Its key elements included wide dispersion of digital technology and computational power at both large and small scales.

This new shift, The Fourth Wave, is usually described as the chaotic but rapidly emerging world of the Internet of Things (IOT), artificial intelligence, 3D printing, robotics. social media, and dozens of other advancements, technologies that are changing the way most of humanity lives and acts every day.

As a result, we could see clearly that the role of technologically-driven leadership was more important than ever in both business and society at large. As this is written, the COVID-19 pandemic is poised to be the most significant disruption of human activity since World War II. For the third time in 20 years, Rob and Mike found themselves discussing a major disturbance in the normal affairs of the world.

In the 2008 economic collapse, trillions of dollars of financial value evaporated in just a few months, and, as the COVID-19 pandemic progresses, a similar or even greater deterioration in the financial worth of the world's largest firms as well as individual income for most is again underway. And, in 2020, even that kind of economic damage doesn't include the ever-growing list of those who have—and may in the future—succumb to the COVID-19 pandemic.

Can people at the top handle that kind of stress? Do they have the talent, wisdom and fortitude to keep their organizations focused and engaged, even as everyone else worries about losing their jobs, their life savings, and perhaps their lives?

Pushed by the world's overloaded crisis agenda—cycles of financial meltdown and recovery, global warming, biological threats, and geopolitical instability—we need to look with fresh eyes at what really matters in our world. Now more than ever, it seems clear that if we pay closer attention to our families, our communities and our personal well-being as well as our jobs, we'll not only be better leaders but better people.

So, we decided to rework *Balanced Leadership for Unbalanced Times* for 2020. Of course, many of the ideas remain timeless; human nature hasn't undergone a complete metamorphosis. However, the specific details of how these enduring notions impact leadership in technical organizations *is* changing, and we've tried to show how these principles are evolving.

We are now ready to share with you the insight that we've gained from a combined 90 years of experience in the world of business.

As a final note, as Rob did in *Balanced Leadership in Unbalanced Times*, we have developed exercises that you can complete to practice these principles. We both recommend you read that book, too. There is some intentional overlap, but there are insights and self-help exercises in Rob's book that aren't here. In this book, we've developed a Personal Leadership Development plan that you can complete—and update regularly—to help you grow and develop as a leader.

INTRODUCTION:

Can Engineers Be Great Leaders?

Leadership in a technically focused company or organization creates unique challenges. The leadership pipeline, quite justifiably, is made up of technologists and engineers.

In the 20th century, three major world leaders were also engineers:

> -Herbert Hoover, a mining engineer, presided over the century's greatest financial implosion and the start of the Great Depression.
>
> -Leonid Brezhnev, a metallurgical engineer, led the Soviet Union into decline and eventual disintegration—his time as leader of the USSR is called the "Brezhnev Stagnation" by some historians.
>
> -Jimmy Carter, a nuclear engineer, was arguably the least effective (or worst) American president since—you guessed it—Herbert Hoover.

Why have these engineers been dismal leaders? Perhaps their technical training and previous technical successes undermined their leadership actions.

Engineers tend to approach things with a logical, deductive mind-set. They tend to believe that if an idea or a program seems rational and clearly defined, then things will, somehow, turn out well. Too often, leaders in technical organizations put too much emphasis on *tasks* but fail to consider the *relationships* that exist between the people who are associated with the work—both those in the workplace and those outside of the workplace. We will explore this idea more in "Understanding Balance" in Chapter One.

In this book, we will offer dozens of strategies for boosting your leadership potential and building a strong and durable balance between tasks and relationships. You can start by creating a detailed personal plan that can help you become a balanced leader—that's our goal in the first four chapters of this book. It's a starting point for the rest of the book, where we discuss proven concepts we are sure you can use to set yourself on a path to a more rewarding life.

Because, you see, we share a passion, just like anyone else who aspires to be a successful leader. By improving the lives of those we interact with, we strive to build wealth and personal contentment for people throughout the world. We also believe that by building wealth, improving personal satisfaction and spreading joy, we aid the quest for world peace. We believe that prosperity and individual fulfillment makes humanity less likely to engage in threats, violence, and warfare. With the strains that exist in the world today, we are more devoted to this than ever.

How Did We Get to Where We Are?

The literature of leadership is ancient and rich:

- The Book of Exodus from the Bible (1400 BC)
- Sun-Tzu's *The Art of War* (500 BC)
- Plato's *Republic* (380 BC), and
- Machiavelli's *The Prince* (1513).

Today, there are hundreds of university programs in the United States that focus on leadership. In these turbulent times, every online news site carries leadership advice. Some of these are helpful, but many are superficial.

As the 21st century began, two conclusions from academic studies stood out:

1. The "endless accumulation of empirical data has not produced an integrated understanding of leadership," Ralph M. Stogdill *The Handbook of Leadership,* 1974.
2. Leadership is situational and relational—it changes depending on the people and the conditions that are present—and there's no particular pattern that can be discerned, James MacGregor Burns, 1985.

Both of these commentaries echo one of Sun-Tzu's observations:

> "Do not repeat the tactics which have gained you one victory, but let your methods be regulated by the infinite variety of circumstances."

Over a combined 90 years of study and work, we have found these two factors in outstanding leaders:

- Great leaders share a passion: They want to make a difference in the world.
- Great leaders constantly strive to strike a balance between work and the other realms of their lives.

It sounds too simple to be correct, yet we've found that these things go hand in hand. The most successful leaders are the ones who work the hardest at balancing all aspects of their lives. And when they do, they find that they really do change the world around them. Sometimes, they deeply affect the course of human history.

What Do We Mean by Balanced Leadership?

We've found that there are 23 noteworthy principles that define a balanced Fourth Wave leader, and that these principles can be divided into 5 major categories:

You know who you are…

- You practice self-reflection
- You recognize and manage your blind spots
- You leverage your strengths while managing your weaknesses
- You take chances and make mistakes
- You acknowledge your mistakes
- You learn from your mistakes
- You maintain a good sense of humor

You consistently demonstrate self-control…

- You manage your time

- You adhere to your values
- You maintain your emotional composure
- You alternate periods of hard work with periods of sustained rest and recreation

Your enthusiasm springs from within…

- You manage your energy
- You keep an optimistic outlook while remaining realistic
- You play as hard as you work

You can put yourself in the other person's shoes…

- You balance your needs with those of others in your organization
- You balance your needs with those of others in your family
- You cultivate consistency while being adaptable to change
- You try to see yourself as others see you

You know how to interact in a group setting and how to benefit from this ability…

- You cultivate a circle of friends and relatives to keep you on the right path
- You continually develop your ability to communicate with others

- You find ways to persuade and influence others without dominating
- You know how to build and lead teams
- You never do any of this alone

In the stormy times we face, it's more important than ever to practice these principles. The mark of a great leader is the ability to lead in all kinds of circumstances. In the toughest of times, leaders need to stand on a rock-solid set of core values.

Larry Bossidy, former chairman at both Honeywell and AlliedSignal explained this quite clearly—he often saw people who did a great job when things are going well, but then fell apart when the going gets tough. But he also observed people who thrived when things were at their worst, but then become so paranoid when then environment improves that they couldn't take advantage of good times. His summary:

> "I always look for someone who can thrive in either circumstance, and I'm amazed at the number of people can't."

And here's something else to keep in mind: Life is almost *always* unbalanced, out of kilter, listing or leaning in one direction or another. Sometimes it's on a global scale; sometimes it's much closer to home. Too many people—and again, engineers in particular—are looking for that magical opportunity where pressure and risk balance perfectly with excitement and reward.

That kind of thinking is delusional—the only time you can experience that sort of balance is for a brief time when the business cycle is on the upswing, and your personal life is going just as you dreamed. Soon, though, you then pass right through it as the pace of work becomes overheated and crazy or something negative happens in your personal life. You can also experience it on the way down when things are slowing down—but the crash of disaster is always just around the corner. Life is dynamic, not static.

The major crises that the world has seen in the past two decades proves that beyond doubt.

You can't stay in that "happy place" for more than a short time. As it says in Ecclesiastes 3:1—and Pete Seeger and the Byrds then sang—"To everything there is a season, and a time to every purpose under heaven." You really can't be a Fourth Wave leader unless you can maintain that balance in every season, through the good as well as the bad.

Finally, it's never too late to polish the skills that will help you grow, prosper, and enjoy life. If you're not an active learner, you can never hope to be a great leader. Nonetheless, there's good news, here, too. There's plenty of solid research that says you can learn how to balance your life, regardless of your innate tendencies. A hard-core engineer can learn to be a better leader while still preserving the analytical skills that made him or her successful in the technical world.

We hope you will use this book to achieve that.

Our World Needs Balanced Leadership

In the past 50 years, engineers and technologists have made an incredible impact on lives around the world. We have medical equipment, transportation options, entertainment, communication, comfort, and food delivery systems that would have been the envy of any pharaoh, king or emperor.

In many ways, though, modern society struggles to manage all of this. Certainly, the free flow of ideas and competing businesses have, in a dance of conflicting outcomes, achieved many great things for the human race.

We believe that we can do better. Mike and Rob have lived through an era of growth in technology that is almost beyond comprehension. And, with the changes that are on the horizon, even greater benefit may be at our doorstep with the advent of the Fourth Wave of the Industrial Revolution.

Technology has achieved many great things for the human race. Yet there are many unexpected and negative aspects. Social media promised and delivered a new and better-connected world, but has also spread deliberate deception, fraud, and criminal enterprises. Autonomous vehicles and artificial intelligence promise even more benefits yet threaten us with potentially ominous outcomes. In a dance of conflicting results, technological gains have also created a world-wide system that is uneven, wasteful of natural resources, and stressful for both humanity and the global environment.

Prometheus brought fire to mankind, and that fire has been both a boon and a threat.

Would higher quality leadership from engineers and technologists have avoided or mitigated some of the crises we've lived through in the past few decades? It's impossible to say.

Yet, technological experts cannot be passive creators of this world. Instead, they must also lead us. Equipping future generations of engineers with capable and balanced leadership skills will drive the equilibrium of benefits and drawbacks toward better outcomes.

As a final comment on why we think this book is important, we need to emphasize that the journey to balanced leadership is neither simple nor instantaneous. In writing this book, Mike and Rob have read dozens or even hundreds of short web notes that are often called "life hacks"—five ways to do this, four key points to do that.

After reading as many of these as we could, we've seen that some of these hacks are valuable (some may be echoed in this book), but most are superficial. Even the most useful suggest that you can modify your habits quickly with simple advice. And, in most cases, these hacks are not supported by research or meaningful historical evidence.

We both know, from the hard knocks of a combined 90 plus years of experience, that cursory changes are rarely (almost never) sufficient to make a meaningful difference in someone's life.

It takes time and significant effort to become a more balanced, more emotionally intelligent leader. This book is structured to help you do that. However, it isn't something you can read through quickly and walk away from without serious reflection and effort.

We've both tried that approach. Plainly and simply, it doesn't work.

We believe that the ideas <u>as well as the suggested self-directed activities</u> in this book can help you make deep, powerful, and enduring changes in your career and your life. We have spent many, many hours trying to create the information and structure that can lead you to that kind of outcome, but, in the end, the burden is on you, the reader, to make the effort.

And that is part of what is necessary to become a highly influential Fourth Wave leader.

The Personal Leadership Development Plan

To help you work through the issues we'll describe in this book, Rob and Mike have developed a spreadsheet to assist you with both self-assessment and planning. This EXCEL workbook (It's also available in Google Sheet format) will help you summarize and track the work you can do after Chapters 3-8. (Chapters 1 and 2 are introductory information you'll need to help sort through the remainder of the book.)

The workbook has these worksheets:

- Summary Plan
- Step A: Forever (To be completed after reading Chapter 3)
- Step B: Foundation Matrix
- Step C: Strategic Goals
- Step D: Intermediate Goals
- Step E: Short-Term Goals
- Step F: Balance Goals
- Five "Action Plan" Worksheets

As you complete each of these worksheets, the "Summary Plan" sheet will automatically be filled in. This Summary Plan will become your Personal Leadership Development plan, and we'll explain how to use this at the end of the book.

You can download a blank workbook by going to **robpasick.com** and looking for the download link in the lower right-hand corner of the home page. You can select either an Excel version or a Google version.

Of course, we believe you will still find this book valuable if you don't choose to use this planning tool, and we know many who read the book will make that choice. Nevertheless, we do believe, based on our own experiences, that using this planning tool will increase the value of this book to you greatly.

No matter which choice you make, we thank you for your time and interest in our ideas.

CHAPTER ONE

Understanding Balance

What do we mean by balance? It will be easier to appreciate this with a simple model. Balanced leadership means a balance of tasks and relationship—and this balance has to extend to your superiors, subordinates, peers, and those you don't work with. And that means family, friends, neighbors, and the wider community, too.

In short, a balanced approach to leadership will keep task-oriented issues in approximate equilibrium with the relationships you maintain with those around you. This is not only a simple idea, it's a very old concept.

In Chinese and Korean philosophy, yin and yang are two opposing yet interdependent forces. Yin is associated with the soft, slow and subtle or hidden aspects of the world, typically shown as dark, while yang is hard, fast, and apparent, shown as light. Yet neither is complete without the other, and both constantly interact in a changing, vibrant mix. In the diagram, both are shown as halves of a whole, each with the seed of the other inside it.

So it is with tasks and relationship in a technical organization. If you choose to focus on tasks to the exclusion of the relationships you have with other people, you will soon find that your ability to accomplish anything in a team setting grinds to a halt. Conversely, if you focus too much on relationships, you will find that nothing is ever accomplished.

In either case, your organization—or at a minimum, your job—will be completely unproductive. Eventually, one or the other will dominate to the detriment of the other.

The best way to think about balancing tasks and relationship is a bit different from the classic yin and yang philosophy. In our view, we think that the tasks of your work <u>rest upon</u> the foundations of relationships. This means the yin-yang arrangement is horizontal, rather than vertical:

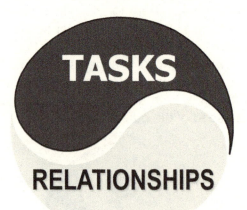

The importance of this isn't trivial—if you don't build sound relationships with those around you, your ability to get any task completed will eventually be impaired. The difficult part is trying to understand the dynamic nature of the balance. It's always changing and never the same—and technical people in particular find this endlessly frustrating. Still, if you destroy the foundation, your relationships with others, you will also destroy your accomplishment of tasks.

In the short term, it's possible to ignore this and still appear successful. One of us (Mike) is an engineer by training and temperament. He will readily admit that he grew up in a working environment and business culture where the motto was, "Do whatever it takes, and just get it done." As he likes to put it, "I was trained to kick butts and take names, and if you got in my way, I made sure you didn't stay there long. Or I just went around you, which was often even more disruptive than confrontation."

In today's workplace, the old-style command-and-control approach wears thin quickly, particularly with engineers who have graduated from university programs in the last thirty years or so. These young adults are usually better educated than their superiors and have access to a vast network of information. When Rob and Mike were in their forties, you could spend a month in the Library of Congress and not learn as much as you can now learn in 60 minutes with a good search engine and a fast broadband connection.

While there will be times and places where the grand vision of extraordinary leadership leaves a great and indelible mark in history, the daily activities that most of us are involved in are not like that at all. All the same, the sum of the things that most of us do is, in fact, leaving a huge collective mark on the human story. Never before have so many well educated, highly motivated, and well-informed people attempted to work together on the complex projects that underpin modern technological societies.

That Doesn't Mean It's Easy to Stay Balanced

When Rob's kids were teenagers, he got really caught up in writing books, and had a fair degree of success. He confesses that he began to act as though his career as an author was more important than his family, and he became obsessed with traveling and giving workshops and figuring out what his next book was going to be about.

One spring, he'd scheduled a great family vacation to Hilton Head in South Carolina. Three days into the trip, his assistant called to say, "You got a call from Oprah. They have an opening on the show and they want you to be on it." Of course, this was an immediate opening, and would require leaving his family in South Carolina while he headed for Chicago.

Without hesitating, Rob booked the trip. Later, he told his wife how excited he was. She was gracious about the whole affair—she even helped Rob buy a new suit to wear on the show—but Rob admits he didn't think twice about leaving the family for the chance to plug his book on Oprah's show.

It was not until he returned a few days later that Rob realized he was so caught up in the task of promoting his books that had neglected his all-important relationship with his wife and children. As Rob puts it,

> "I'd done a lot of things in my life, but the fact that I was on Oprah was special. People started calling me "Oprah Man" and asking me what Oprah was like. I'm not ashamed to admit that it went straight to my head. I was seduced by success. It was amazing how easy it was for me to set aside some of my basic values. And the irony of it, of course, was that the book I was promoting on Oprah's show was about how men should shed their

> domineering, self-centered behavior. I was becoming a case study for my own book!"

It took a while, but eventually he came to his senses. The demands of family and daily life forced Rob to reset his priorities. In fact, Rob didn't write another book for several years, due in large part to the realization that it was time to back off.

Now, let's step back and think about the consequences of that very imbalance. Rob was highly focused on task, to the detriment of relationships. Being perceptive, he eventually noticed before he faced a more critical problem—perhaps the breakup of his family relationships—and changed his ways. But to react, he had to give up on tasks for some period of time and didn't do much in his quest to become a well-respected author for a relatively long time. So again, he was lacking balance, and there was a price to be paid.

We're happy to say that Rob now believes he has restored and maintained that balance for many years, but it's a reminder that it's easy to fall into imbalance and not easy at all to get back to a well-adjusted position once things go awry.

Inside an Engineer's Head

For the past fifty years, Paramount's *Star Trek* franchise has been a favorite with technical people. After all, the various incarnations of *Star Trek* all have a key character who is an engineer. These engineers pull amazing, semi-scientific rabbits out of their hats and save the day with improbable, pseudo-technical feats of intelligence blended with courageous, even daring leadership.

But more than any other character, tech heads gravitate to Mr. Spock and the other Vulcans that populate the franchise. As extra-terrestrials, Vulcans are race of completely dispassionate, logical, and rational beings who suppress their raging emotional sentiments to pursue specific and coherent goals and objectives. Spock is all task—he cares (or so he says) not a whit about relationships. In one of the original series' famous quotes, Spock says,

> "I fail to comprehend your indignation, sir. I have simply made the logical deduction that you are a liar."

Now, think about your last meeting. Did you expect everyone to behave rationally, to tell the truth, to make their points and raise issues logically and reasonably? Of course you did! And, of course you were disappointed. You were disappointed because *Vulcans are television make-believe*.

Human beings don't behave that way very often. The only human beings who fail to react to the moment-by-moment activities around them with emotional responses are people who have severe brain injuries—and such people also suffer from severely degraded problem-solving capability and other cognitive flaws.

You may resist your emotional side because you may perceive it as weakness. Reacting emotionally can undermine you professionally. Most of us have had the distinctly unsettling experience of reacting to something that was said in a meeting with a cruel or nasty retort, or perhaps an angry outburst. After the ugly episode has passed, you may find yourself asking "Why did I do that? It was foolish and counter-productive, but the comment just jumped out of my brain into my mouth."

To understand this better, we need to know a few things about how the human brain functions.

First, when you speak, several areas in the brain have to work in concert. Ultimately, your brain thinks the thoughts and controls the physical mechanisms of speech (breath, lips, tongue). Using neurological scanning techniques, scientists have mapped the sequence of action in various brain centers when you speak.

Research suggests that even when speech is fairly deliberate, the mechanical control centers of the brain <u>fire before the cognitive elements</u> of the brain are activated. It's actually true: *you usually speak before you think*.

Ultimately, our most fundamental responses, such as the fight-or-flight response that keeps us alive in unpredictable situations, are found in an ancient part of our brain, a part that closely resembles the entire brain of a reptile. Neurophysiologists call this the "R-complex." It is also believed to be the most primitive evolutionary part of the brain, and it includes the motor function areas—areas that control the first actions of speaking.

The fight-or-flight response is mediated, or over-ridden, by the intellectual capabilities of the human brain most of the time. But when we feel threatened or endangered, your inner-alligator rises up and before the conscious elements of thought can intervene, you blurt out an insult, an attack, or something insensitive or inflammatory.

This is more likely to happen when stress and the associated stakes of the game are high. When things really matter and the pressure is on, the inner-alligator strikes out and damages your long-term working relationship with someone else. The offended party may then find that his or her inner-alligator *also* strikes out. If neither one of you responds with flight rather than fight, we can only hope that cooler heads will prevail. But both Rob and Mike have observed these situations in business settings, and in a few cases they moved to the edge of violent confrontation.

Engineers and technical people, expecting logical and detached behavior, often trigger their own or their team's inner alligators. Driven by simple and clear-cut task considerations, an inner alligator may rise to the top and crush a relationship with someone or possibly even everyone within earshot..

We are humans, not Vulcans, and while emotions may undermine us, they provide important data about situations, ourselves, and our teams. Attending to our own emotions and those of our team is part of the never-ending balance of tasks and relationship that is leadership.

Leaving Footprints

More and more business leaders are looking for tools to help them deal with the every-increasing demands on their time and energy. Like most of us, they must keep four or five balls in the air and live in fear that if they drop one, all will tumble down.

Yet with tasks, if we fail by not meeting a deadline or completing an assignment correctly, we'll often recover in time, sometimes spectacularly so. We also forget that if we drop the ball in our relationships, we may not bounce back so easily.

Engineers don't have a good track record in this area. Traditionally, tech heads focus heavily on task, but the technical culture is changing. More engineers are now rejecting the idea that work is everything and that getting something done in your job is worth almost any consequence.

Just as people now care about their "carbon footprint," the impact of humans on the environment in terms of the production of greenhouse gases, we find that people also are worrying more and more about their personal footprints. They're asking, "What will I leave behind? Will my life have any significance?" Too often, clumsy personal relationships diminish our imprint on the human existence.

The story of Robert Kearns and the battle over his invention of interval windshield wipers illustrates how poor balance can diminish the footprint you leave behind. This story is told in the movie *Flash of Genius.* Kearns' invention was clearly a stroke of genius, and it's likely that major automakers appropriated his idea without compensation or intellectual credit. Kearns became obsessed with this, and it eventually dominated the end of his life.

To those who knew Kearns personally, he was not the man depicted in the movie. He was a dynamic and truly wonderful man, with incredible charm. But all of that evaporated as he lost his psychological balance during his legal struggles with Ford and Chrysler. Eventually, his marriage soured, some of his children abandoned him, and he had physical and emotional breakdowns. Prior to the movie, Kearns was forgotten except to those who knew him personally.

The desire to leave something behind is deeply ingrained in most people. In many ways, this drive is part of what inspires young people to take up engineering. However, in the dynamic world of the 21st century, the lone wolf inventor is really an anachronism. Turning a good idea into reality simply can't be done by solo operators. The level of technology in the world today is simply too multifaceted for a loner to have much of an effect.

Making an impact requires the combined efforts of many people in the present-day technical arena. Teams must collaborate productively and robustly.

Of course, it's true—you can get something done *once* by behaving in a rude or domineering fashion, but your ability to repeat your success will be badly wounded. It might even be fatally wounded, particularly in the world of electronically based social networking where people are willing to post on Twitter, Instagram, Reddit, or dash off an instant message about every aspect of their life, including the hurts and mental slings and arrows they suffer.

How can you avoid these pitfalls?

CHAPTER TWO

Establish Your Balance Points

Real leaders understand that it's not enough just to have a title on the door. They want to create great products or services, and exert influence in civic life, or in a faith-based movement or perhaps in a social network. They work hard to sustain a strong interpersonal or family structure and know that caring for their personal physical and emotional well-being is critical to achieving any and all of these objectives.

But that's just a description of what makes a leader successful. We haven't really answered a more basic question: what *is* a leader?

The word "leader" doesn't even appear in the English language until sometime in the mid-14th century. It's derived from the old English term "leden" meaning "to show the way." If you look in a dictionary, you can find a bewildering number of definitions for the term—one of our favorites is "a horse placed in advance of others."

Peter Drucker, perhaps the most influential student of leadership in the 20th century, put forth a simpler idea. A leader is one who has followers—one who influences others. It's not about the title or role that anyone might have, it's about how they affect the behavior of those around them.

We think that's a critical idea. And, no matter what the setting, it's important for leaders to be in tune with others. In the wild, a lone wolf has a short life span. Living in a competitive environment without the support of the pack shortens your time on earth. This is particularly relevant in the world of technology, where dozens, hundreds, or even thousands of people must work cooperatively to bring ideas to fruition. A wolf, working alone, simply cannot kill the prey needed for survival. A solo engineer can't make much of an impact, either.

Effective leaders during the Fourth Wave need to be multidimensional. They're not obsessives who do nothing but work for the bottom line or personal gain. While they are almost always energetic and driven, they also are able to shift their focus fluidly from one arena to the next. A great leader might be able to jump from a complex equation to counseling a subordinate—and then find themselves deep in a financial analysis the following hour.

This isn't natural for those most interested in technical achievements. Engineers are often disinterested in persuading others, and some even think that "selling" their idea is beneath their dignity. This is the same as a wolf believing he can kill a moose without pack mates.

In almost every organization that has a deep technical base, we have observed that engineers put forth imaginative ideas and occasionally incredible proposals. However, these concepts are seldom well rounded; they focus on technological aspects, and don't often consider social and economic facets of the idea. As a result, great ideas flounder and fail, as senior managers and executives—who are rarely engineers—see the weaknesses in these other areas. In the end, engineers often slink off to a corner and sulk, grousing that "management just doesn't get it."

That's _not_ effective leadership!

As famed sci-fi author Robert A. Heinlein noted, many people predicted the technological development of the automobile—but not one person predicted the change in human mating habits that the automobile eventually fostered. Prior to widespread auto ownership, courtship in

America was a tightly controlled experience, with most young couples paired off between bordering farm families or neighborhood acquaintances. Privacy during courtship consisted of a swing on the front porch. A large backseat mounted on a set of self-propelled wheels changed that dramatically as the pool of potential mates and the opportunities for private encounters expanded beyond anyone's imagination.

People who are able to synthesize the broader aspects of an important idea work intensely but they also play and rest intensely. They get things accomplished, but they don't expend all of their energy in one area to the detriment of others. And they don't try to do everything at once. They may not balance out every day, but they do achieve stability over time.

Ways to Ease the Way

Regis McKenna, a Silicon Valley leader who helped launch Apple, Genentech, Electronic Arts, Intel, and 3Com—among many others—has said "It is ironic that in this age of electronic communication, personal interaction is becoming more important than ever."

Here are some ideas about communication and interactions that can help you achieve more balance in your organization—and your life.

To move fluidly between activities and ideas, you need to be wary of transition points

- Transition points occur when you start and end your workday, when you move from your cubical or office into a meeting, or when you embark on a trip. This can also arise when a new message comes through on Slack,

Discord, WhatsApp, or some other "instant" source. These are times when technical people are most likely to allow the fight-or-flight response to interfere with relationships because their brain is still seething with conscious ideas from the latest things you've been doing. You need to have some specific activities to reduce the driving forces that can cause problems.

- Try and develop a plan for each day. We're not advocating a specific to-do list (which is useful), but instead that you have a broad agenda. This might only be in your head, but you might benefit from writing out two or three lines about what you want to accomplish *today*. This can be done during your commute, or, better yet, done at your desk by arriving 20-30 minutes early each day. When you arrive early, you often get a degree of privacy and relief from stress that makes clear thinking easier.

- The same principle applies when you are returning home—use your commute time to think about the two or three things that you think will add the most to your life away from work that day. During a period of "stay home" orders, setting aside a period to decompress when working from home would be equally beneficial. Most engineers would specifically gain from thinking about how they will relate to their partner and their children that day.

- Too often, people move from meeting to meeting without any time between sessions. If possible, see if you can schedule 30 minutes between meetings—particularly for important meetings. Then, use that 30-minute time frame to think through the specific behaviors that you want to exhibit during the meeting. Don't say you can't do this; once you've accepted a meeting invite on Outlook or other app, you can block out the 30 minutes on one or both sides of the accepted meeting, leaving time to prepare for another meeting. Sometimes, you won't be able to do that, but you will be surprised how often you will reduce stress simply via preparation.

- For example, before you hit the road for a business trip, make sure you planned the travel arrangements carefully. Some surprises are likely on almost every trip, but the web makes it possible to learn a great deal about your flight, the city you will visit (even the smallest rural town seems to have their own web site these days), the hotel you will stay in, and the restaurants you might consider. If you do this, you can reduce the stress of travel and retain more energy and, more importantly, emotional equilibrium when you are engaged in working on the road.

Beware of the email-instant message-social media trap

- If there's one thing we see that creates task-relationship balance problems, it's the all-consuming pressure everyone feels to respond instantaneously to every request, every comment, and every communication we receive. There's a simple fact underlying all of this noise we are immersed in every day: not all of it can possibly be that important.

- Unless physical safety or imminent financial risk is present, you really ought to rethink your minute-by-minute priorities. If you are going to find time to achieve steadiness in your life, you aren't likely to be able to do that if you are addicted to email or instant messaging. How many times have you responded immediately to a less-than-urgent email only to realize you have "flamed" someone or —or worse, you completely misread or misunderstood the original message. Take the time needed for a calm and collected approach to electronic communication.

Sometimes you just have to be realistic and accept that you can't do everything you would like to do—or even need to do.

- This is another symptom of the "everything is critical" syndrome. There is an extraordinarily high probability that the sun <u>will</u> rise tomorrow, no matter what *you* do. The feeling that so many engineers have that every detail, every assignment is critical is quite likely to lead to excessive emphasis on tasks, with a corresponding de-emphasis on relationships. Perfectionism is a deadly disease, one that can eventually destroy your effectiveness and even have a profoundly negative impact on your health.

- Even the President of the United States can't respond to every major crisis in the same way. Most veterans of the West Wing have admitted that they really could deal with two or at most three key issues at any moment in time. This meant that they had to defer action or even ignore potentially earth-shaking events and pressures in order to address other potential doomsday scenarios.

- When sorting through priorities, avoid the trap of excluding fun and non-essential activities. The saying "all work and no play makes Jack a dull boy" is as true today as ever. On the other hand—balance is important—the rest of the rhyme is rarely quoted: "All play and no work make Jack a mere toy."

Like astronaut Neil Armstrong, who took one small step on the moon in 1969, take some small steps that can lead to big results

- Planning guru Alan Lakein, author of "How to Get Control of Your Time and Life," advocates using the five-minute rule if you can't seem to get started on a project.

Set a timer for five minutes and work on the project. When the timer goes off, move on to something else or set the timer for another five minutes. Lakein says most people keep going for much more than five minutes.

- Rob often counsels his clients to identify the time of day when they do their most creative work, then keep that time free of meetings or distractions. Mike has taken that advice personally and found that it helped him be both more productive—and aided him in controlling his inner alligator. "Getting real work done on a regular basis, even when I'm pulled in many directions at once, often keeps me from responding to things with a hard, gut-level reaction," he admits.

When in doubt, ask questions

- If you think you know everything, it's likely that you probably know next to nothing. Those around you are nearly always willing to help you with advice and assistance, but you *must have the courage to ask—and then have the drive to use good advice whenever you get it.*

- Asking reasonable and sound questions builds relationships. By asking questions, you signal to others that you trust them and that you need their assistance in life. And, if you incorporate their suggestions in your work, you will have an automatic ally in the implementation of any plan—particularly since it's an improved plan that bears another person's imprint. Since most great ideas fail during implementation, often due to a lack of wide-ranging support in an organization, this is no small thing.

- Even outside of your career, asking others for advice and support develops strong bonds and long-term networks of friends. Humans are social animals, and the daily affairs of living are more pleasurable and more rewarding when shared with friends and family.

Take a closer look at what's driving your bus

- In an article in *Science*, researchers reported on their study of envy. If you feel hostility or a sense of unfairness because others have what you lack—including beauty, a large home, a promotion or the admiration of peers—you are suffering from envy. What's worse is that feelings of envy activate the same brain centers associated with physical pain. On the flip side, when subjects imagined the failure of those they envied, the *pleasure centers of their brains were activated*. These are terribly unbalanced reactions, and the taste of pleasure caused by this desire to see others fall short can easily spur a nasty personal encounter with someone you envy. There's even a word for this in German: *schadenfreude*, meaning "pleasure derived from another's failure."

- Engineers can find themselves consumed with these emotions. After all, they leave college with the highest starting salaries of almost any bachelor's degree program. They know they have studied a very difficult and extremely challenging curriculum. But, after ten years or so, they see lawyers, financial accountants, and even liberal arts majors earning more, buying bigger houses, and fancier cars. This often drives envy, and the emotion is destructive.

- Technical people who fall into this trap need to step back and be honest. If they are, they will inevitably recognize that the unfairness they perceive is of their own making. Their own inability to keep tasks and relationship in a symmetrical arrangement is often the underlying factor in these situations, and this is well within their ability to change.

Teamwork Works

If you are less likely to succeed as a lone wolf, that means you have to work with others. Recognizing the importance of your team also will give you the balance of tasks and relationship that is so valuable. Failing to recognize your limits can be your undoing. Working with a team will keep an overinflated sense of how powerful and important you are from taking over.

In American culture, we love to associate the idea of business teams with sports teams. Again, the excitement and heroic nature of a champion is loved by almost everyone—just consider what happens when the Super Bowl, the World Series, or March Madness rolls around.

But what kind of team will you be on? When Mike was in high school, he lettered in three sports: football, basketball, and golf.

In team golf, you simply add your scores. In fact, in many places, it's against high school rules to assist your teammates. "Giving advice" is a two-shot penalty, which is fairly severe in a short nine-hole contest. Interaction and assistance is literally banned.

Unfortunately, too many teams involving engineers work like golf teams. "Mark does X, Jill does Y, and Yusuf does Z. Then we'll all be done." Make no mistake, that's better than Mark doing all the work. However, there's no synergy and no cross-fertilization that might turn a mundane result into a great one. Of course, tech heads are often comfortable in this situation because it doesn't require that they invest any psychic energy into balancing tasks with relationships. "Just tell me exactly what you want and I'll get it done" is a sentiment that you can often hear.

Nevertheless, the work just can't ever be divided so cleanly, so neatly, and so effectively that independent, non-interactive task-focused work *alone* can provide a high-level result.

Basketball requires more cooperation, but almost anyone who follows basketball knows that the teams with the best one or two players usually win more than other teams. Stars make all the difference, and a great player, like the late Kobe Bryant, Michael Jordan, or LeBron James, can make average teammates look great.

The "star" model doesn't work well in business over time. Sure, a team with a superstar over-achiever (who is often out of balance) can generate a spectacular success in any given situation. Sooner rather than later, though, this will come unglued, as the superstar wants to have the ball all the time. In business—or at home—this isn't a sustainable way forward.

There's an important role for everyone off the basketball court, and the egoism of a superstar and the dependency of a team on that superstar doesn't seem to work well in either business or private life. Even when this brings short term triumph, it rarely brings repeated success. Mike and Rob have seen a number of companies where too many talented "stars" got in each other's way and ruined daily activities. Once again, tasks and relationship are no longer combined in the way yin and yang must be for the best result.

Finally, football is a game that requires each and every player to execute well on every play and in full coordination—or the team will falter and may very well lose.

With 22 players on the field at any moment, it only takes the failure of one participant to doom a team to disaster—and that's much more like the actuality we all face away from any team-based sporting event.

This point was brought home to Rob by Robert Chapman, former president and CEO of United Bancorp Inc. "Leaders may be powerful and extremely important to their companies, but they're also just ordinary people – no better or worse than anyone else," Bob notes.

"If your company or department or project is successful, it's not just because of you – it's because everyone has done their job, including the cleaning crews who came in after you went home at night."

When Mike was 15 years old and a sophomore in high school, he was a bit more than 6 foot tall and weighed 175 pounds—but he was able to make his school's varsity team and got to start in almost every game. With two games left in the season, his coach moved him from defensive end to offensive center. What the coach didn't tell him was that the defensive nose guard for the other team—the center's main opponent—was 19 years old, stood 6 foot 7 inches tall, and weighed 270 pounds. That "other guy" was named Dave Pureifory, who later was an All-American star at Eastern Michigan University and then played 11 years in the NFL as a defensive lineman.

Needless to say, Pureifory simply dominated the game. Mike's team lost 55-0 (or something similar—he really can't remember many of the details since he was pounded senseless) and Pureifory completely disrupted Mike's team's offense (and Mike's physical well-being, too). In this case, regardless of how well others did, the unglamorous job of center was pivotal, and a shortcoming in that contribution was fatal to the team's chances for victory.

With the passage of time, Mike has also realized another facet of this beating. His coach and teammates gave him no assistance—they never double-teamed the guy who was literally beating his brains in—and he wasn't even warned about what he faced. All of this was far short of what a team should be, and the results reflected this deficit in shared or balanced responsibility.

So, if balance and teamwork are so important, how can you build skills and habits that will lead to the equilibrium that is critical to achievement in these crazy, stressful times?

CHAPTER THREE

Build on Your Strengths

If you've read this far, you are probably interested in altering the way you balance tasks and relationships in your life and your career. Now comes the hard part: you have to modify some of your behaviors. If our experiences are any guide, and both Mike and Rob have seen a great deal of this in our lives, there's good news and bad news for you.

The good news is that you can start by building on your strengths. Everyone has a unique set of strengths and abilities, and the more time you spend using these unique talents, the more successful and satisfied you're likely to be.

The bad news is that you will have to face up to some aspects of your behavior that aren't helping you remain steady. Engineers in particular often seem to think that building stronger, more interactive links with other people is manipulative, that ideas alone matter. By starting with a better understanding of the things that give you strength, you will be better prepared.

Still, during this journey, you will, almost without question, experience moments of doubt and possibly even shame. If you don't feel awkward at some point, you probably aren't going to improve your lot in the world. A plant can't grow and develop unless it changes. A child can't become an adult without undergoing a huge amount of physical change—but an even greater amount of personal, psychological change.

If you had a wonderful childhood, a thoroughly enjoyable adolescence, and are now a happy adult, you are truly fortunate—and you are part of a very, very small minority. Everyone has doubts; everyone worries at one time or another about how they are seen by other people. That's good, because if you never worry about the way others see you, you are almost certainly a very self-centered and probably quite selfish individual, and you are unlikely to ever develop profound leadership skills.

Discover Your Strong Points

When confronted with a complex problem, the most effective way to proceed is nearly always the same—start with the easy part. It's like working a crossword puzzle. If you try to solve a crossword puzzle by taking on the hardest, least obvious clues and longest words, you are likely to get stuck. Instead, the best strategy is to get the easy words first, and then build from there.

In the same way, begin with what's sound and positive about your personality and work habits. Once you've assessed that, you can tackle the things you need to improve.

There are two ways to go about this. The first is to examine yourself. This is the easiest and the one that sets the stage for anything else.

Start out by writing down (yes, writing—OK, doing it on your phone or table is fine) *ten things you think make you a good person*. It could be that you are good with numbers, you are a responsible citizen, you pay your bills on time, or you are kind to dogs and cats — whatever it is, just list ten things. Once you start, you will find this is either easy or difficult. No matter, just write them down. If it's easy, you may have trouble reducing your list down to ten. If it seems difficult, you may have trouble getting to ten. That insight alone makes this a worthwhile exercise.

Why write these ideas out? First, the act of writing requires more organization than just compiling a mental list. Second, actively writing requires your brain to transfer information from one area of the brain to another, and this will force a deeper and more considered look at your own self-image than simply imagining a list. Third, you need to have something to look at and compare as you progress. If you have a mental list, you are unlikely to recall the details of this list in two weeks, let alone over the next decade of your life.

A relatively inexpensive but more structured tool for self-examination is the Internet-based Strengths Finder Profile, created by Donald O. Clifton, Tom Rath and a team of scientists from the Gallup Organization. This team created a Web site (www.strengthsfinder.com) and published a book, "StrengthsFinder 2.0." When you buy the book, you get an access code so you can take the assessment online. The program analyzes your answers and comes up with your five top strengths. Then, it provides action plans and other activities designed to help you maximize your strengths.

If you had trouble doing a self-assessment, or if you think you would benefit from a wider perspective, then gather input from other people. Rob has extensive experience with this through his psychology practice. If you are reticent about asking others for their opinion, don't hesitate to ask yourself <u>why</u> you are reluctant. We think you'll find many people are willing to do this, particularly if you are brief and direct in your request. In fact, doing this—asking for assistance—is one of the skills you need to develop, and this is an undemanding one to help you get started on your journey.

One of the easiest methods was developed by Dan Sullivan, author and founder of the Strategic Coach, who advocates simply sending e-mails to the people who know you best. Explain that you're going through a leadership development process and ask them to describe a few (less than five) of your unique strengths, talents and contributions.

After you've gotten feedback from others, you need to compare what they think and what you wrote down. You might do this on a spreadsheet (techsters usually enjoy creating a tabular view of this stuff), or you might write each idea on an index card and then arrange them in the order you think is most significant.

No matter how you perform this self-examination, you will probably be best served by choosing and then working with the top five strengths that you have identified. It's a comfortable number to handle for goal-setting—too many can become confusing, and fewer than five probably doesn't show enough of who you really are to help you grow.

Once you've done this, enter these key strengths on the "Step A-Forever" worksheet in the Personal Leadership Development workbook.

Pasick Personal Leadership Development Plan
Know Yourself--*Enduring Standards For Personal Behavior*
What Is Your Leadership Baseline?
A. List your 5 Key Strengths *(What are the things you do best?)*
1
2
3
4
5

The next step is to see how your best attributes fit in with your goals.

Draft A Personal Mission Statement

Remember our principles of leadership?

- Great leaders share a passion: They want to make a difference in the world.
- Great leaders constantly strive to strike a balance between work and the other realms of their lives.

What is your passion? What is the difference you want to make? Define where you are going in a personal mission statement.

When engineers think of action, they think about doing something that affects the world around them. This often involves manipulating the natural environment in a way that makes life easier, more pleasant, more entertaining, or all of these at once.

How broad can this be? Henry Ford saw his mission as bringing personal mobility and a better life to the rural farm boys he grew up with. Bill Gates sought to apply computers to improve business and personal lives in fundamentally new ways. Elon Musk wants to push technology and business to the limits of physics.

A real mission is usually so big that it's rarely finished. It's also an ongoing effort. It isn't just a goal to be achieved. It is more like an expedition – a lifelong trek with an end result that is off in the distant future. Some—probably most—missions can never be completed. Like the Starship Enterprise, with its "continuing mission to explore strange new worlds" the excitement is in seeking and confronting challenges, not in reaching a finish line.

A mission isn't something you make up. To answer the big question, think about what you have been doing all along. Whether you know it or not, you probably have been on a mission already. It may be tied to your work or to some other arena of life.

Rob and Mike have each defined their mission.

For Rob, his daily professional activities are dominated by a simple theme:

> "My mission is to make the world a better place by helping individuals and organizations reach their full potential. I know those are vague terms and the goal is large and immeasurable. Yet, for my whole life, this is what I have been about. It was my mission even before I could conceptualize the notion of a mission."

Mike's mission is somewhat different, but related, and has been evident in his role as a globe-trotting engineer trying to help people and organizations become more efficient and effective:

> "I want to improve companies and build prosperity for people throughout the world. When individuals feel successful and have better material lives, humanity is less likely to engage in threats, violence, and warfare. I understand that this is ultimately unattainable, but over my lifetime I've slowly realized that this idea is central to whatever I have done in my career. We're all better off when we're all a bit richer."

Here are some questions to help you figure out your personal mission statement:

- What am I here on Earth to do?
- What have I been passionate about since I was a young adult?

- What decisions have I made that were affected by my passions?
- What have I accomplished to advance my mission?
- What have I chosen not to do because it conflicted with my passions?

Take some time to consider these questions and then, again, write down your personal mission statement. You can now enter this on the next section of the "Step A-Forever" worksheet.

Pasick Personal Leadership Development Plan
Know Yourself--*Enduring Standards For Personal Behavior*
What Is Your Leadership Baseline?
B. What Is Your Mission *(What are you here on earth to do?)*

Describe Your Vision of Success

A vision and a mission aren't the same thing. A mission is global in scope and never-ending. A vision is a mental picture of success, time-constrained and specific enough so that it can be measured.

To figure out your vision, answer this simple – yet radical – question:

When you're really successful at a point in the future, what will that success look like?

A real vision—as opposed to a wish—has several key ingredients:

- There's a leap-frog objective in your vision—it's not a "me too" accomplishment.
- Your objectives are achievable, not impossible, and they can be compared against meaningful standards of some kind.
- There's a specific time frame for accomplishment (before I'm 40, before I retire, by 2022 or by the end of next month).
- The goal is enduring; this is something you will look back on at a later time and be proud to say "I was part of that."
- It's a benefit to yourself, and to those around you. If this vision relates to your career, the vision will benefit those you work with, both personally and professionally.

A well-known historical example can illustrate how a vision statement should be crafted. In 1961, with Soviet manned space missions orbiting above while American missiles were exploding on the launch pad, President Kennedy stated a simple mission:

- Put a man on the moon—not just put a man into orbit as the Soviet Union had done, but a leapfrog (and inspiring) objective
- By the end of the decade—a definite time frame
- The moon—not Mars—was chosen as a target because Kennedy had queried NASA about what was achievable, given the needed resources and time—and the moon seemed (and has been) a

measurable and enduring standard of real significance

- Bring him back safely—a benefit (at least to astronauts)

Surprisingly, some NASA engineers had seen this final criterion as a secondary goal; after all, test pilots had been routinely killed in crazy airplane designs for as long as man was playing with flight. Why spend extra time and money on this frill? In fact, the first Mercury capsule designs had no windows, and the astronauts had no flight controls; that would be accomplished back on earth. Astronauts called this plan "Spam in a can." At times, the engineering emphasis on tasks at the expense of relationship can be a bit chilling!

At this point, you should now consider how your strengths and mission fit together and try and describe your personal vision of success.

Use the bullet points above as a checklist and the "man on the moon" as an example to see if you can describe something that is a real vision and not just a vague hope. Again, this vision should be something that will fit into just a few lines, perhaps even a single sentence.

You can now record your vision statement on the "Step A-Forever" worksheet.

Tech Leadership 4.0

Pasick Personal Leadership Development Plan
Know Yourself--*Enduring Standards For Personal Behavior*
What Is Your Leadership Baseline?
C. What Is Your Vision? *(Your future picture of success over the next 10 years)*

Define Your Core Values

As you progress in leadership and responsibility, you will be challenged by difficult decisions.

Decisions are easy when the answer is obvious. Many leadership decisions do not have obvious solutions because they involve the analysis of trade-offs between competing risks and benefits.

When the way is unclear, when there is no obvious right answer, which way will you turn? In a world that isn't black and white, how do you evaluate the shades of gray?

Most people, but tech heads in particular underestimate how challenging and difficult this can be as your influence grows.

You won't find it possible to develop a strong set of core values in the middle of emotionally charged decisions that can affect dozens, hundreds, or even thousands of other people. First, make sure you understand what you stand for as part of your personal transformation into a Fourth Wave leader.

Your list of core values should include statements about what you will and will not do in conducting your life. It may be simple things like, "I'm never going to tell people things I know are false" or "I'm always going to respect others." These are the principles you abide by and vow not to compromise, knowing that sooner or later you will be in situations where a course of action isn't clear. These values will guide your actions.

Oprah Winfrey captured the significance of this with these words: "Real integrity is doing the right thing, knowing that nobody's going to know whether you did it or not."

Without core values as a guide, it is easy to lose your way personally and professionally. Enron, an energy company, used unethical accounting schemes to hide financial losses in the late 1990s, culminating in bankruptcy in 2001 and a long prison sentence for its CEO, Jeffrey Skilling. False claims about the technology powering the blood testing company Theranos has led to fraud charges against the company and its CEO, Elizabeth Holmes. These leaders also ensnared many others, who collaborated in ways large and small to enable these schemes. That shows that this kind of behavior can tempt many people, not just a few uber-powerful executives.

By now, you should have some skill in looking at yourself and describing some of your own traits. So, add this list to your pile of written self-assessments: what are the five most important values that drive you?

Rob has an example list that he likes to use to get people started on their own list. Here are some examples of individual core values that he often encounters in working with people:

- Stay true to my faith.

- Show the love I have for the people in my life.
- Encourage people to succeed at their highest values.
- Set the right values for my company and adhere to them.
- Always tell the truth, no matter how difficult.
- Never inflict physical or emotional violence on another human being.
- Recognize the good in others.
- Always uphold my sense of integrity and adhere to my ethics.
- If you're still having trouble with this, think about these words: trustworthy, dependable, reliable, responsible, truthful, honest, consistent, honorable, upright, faithful, conscientious.

That should be enough to get you started. Add the five most important core values that you believe to your self-evaluations on the "Step A-Forever" worksheet.

Pasick Personal Leadership Development Plan
Know Yourself--*Enduring Standards For Personal Behavior*
What Is Your Leadership Baseline?

D. What Are Your Core Values? *(Guiding principles, even when the going gets tough)*
1.
2.
3.
4.
5.

Addressing Those Other Things

At this point, you've started to develop a significant personal file about yourself—you have a list of strengths, a statement of your personal mission, and now a motivating and stimulating vision of specific accomplishments that you want to reach. You've also made a list of the value-based standards that you believe should guide your life.

You have started on the road of self-cognition, which consists of knowing who you are and having a sound understanding of what makes you tick. You should also have a description of the key issues that form your values, the compass that guides toward things you feel underscore your behavior as a responsible adult.

On the flip side, we all have a list of habits and tendencies that hold us back and deter us from ever reaching our vision or fulfilling our mission. Understanding this is also an element of self-awareness. Too often, people who want to improve their lives start by trying to eliminate bad habits: going on a diet, quitting smoking, promising to stop swearing, or giving up some other failing. This isn't easy, as untold number of broken New Year's resolutions prove.

To understand why, we again need to understand a basic psychological principle: reward and punishment are not symmetrical. A reward—something that makes us feel good—is a great way to stimulate and build a new behavior. More importantly, rewards are good at building specific, well-controlled habits and conduct. However, *it's very difficult to create a new behavior through punishment.*

Punishment is effective at eliminating behaviors but it has the distinct drawback that punishment is a very blunt instrument. Punishment often causes people to stop other, unrelated behavior because the avoidance of discomfort or pain is such a strong, primal reaction. Anyone who has been reasonably successful during the challenges of raising adolescent children understands this well.

When Mike's oldest child, Ben, entered middle school he started to have academic problems. He wasn't doing his homework, he didn't participate in class, and, though he was an extremely engaging and likable young teen, he was clearly withdrawing from his teachers. When Mike and his wife Carol were summoned to school to discuss this, Mike did what a lot of fathers would do: he blew his stack.

He threatened Ben with punishment, most notably the elimination of Ben's real passion, playing ice hockey. What was the result? Well, initially, it seemed to be good. Mike and Carol stopped getting notes (this was pre-Internet, in the electronic dark ages) from school, and they felt things must be improving.

Soon enough, they learned otherwise when they got a phone call from the middle school vice-principal asking them to come in for a conference. What they found was that Ben had simply stopped bringing the notes home that he was given by his teachers and was forging Mike's signature on the notes. In other words, *he had stopped another behavior—bringing home the notes—that he felt was causing the pain he had felt when threatened by his father.*

When toddlers do something dangerous, like reaching for a hot stove, you can effectively "extinguish" this behavior with a reprimand. "No!" can be a powerful tool. However, once a child reaches the age of four, their behavior has become sufficiently complex that simple scolding is less effective, and usually will result in the elimination of other behaviors—behaviors that are desirable. It can also foster the development of other behaviors that aren't particularly attractive, such as lying and other deceptive acts.

We've all seen this at work. Sooner or later, management will scold people for not being responsive to emails, spending too much time shopping on-line, or doing something else that's perceived as non-productive and the responses include:

- Grumbling and anger, including destructive gossip and rumor-mongering
- More time spent doing nothing at all
- More time spent prepping resumes or cruising LinkedIn
- Less time spent on productive work—exactly the opposite of what management wanted to achieve

We're certain that none of these were within the realm of things that management thought would happen when they initiated the "punishment" of a mild admonishment.

The better thing to do would be to find ways to reward people for being more productive. This doesn't have to be financial; simple, honest, and sincere praise is usually all it takes. Even better, using a positive reward, such as praise, will be directed at the specific thing that management wants to see: more output at the end of the day.

Why is this important?

Simple—we don't think that dwelling on your faults will be the critical act that helps you attain balance. We think it is generally better to build on your strengths, and, guided by your mission, vision, and values, develop additional strengths. This is much more likely to help you balance tasks and relationships than trying to break some of the bad habits you may have developed in your life.

If you are really busy doing positive, rewarding things you just won't have time to do those negative things that can bring punishment or make you feel guilt. But you do need to be able to recognize when you start falling into bad habits, so you can place more emphasis on doing the right things—the things that are aimed at your mission and vision, supported by your values.

Still in all, anyone who wants to be a Fourth Wave leader needs to know their blind spots—places where their behavior can be erratic or self-defeating. This will make up the last of the five lists we think are necessary to understanding who you are and what you want to accomplish as a leader.

Many of life's problems stem not so much from the things that happen to us as from how we think about and respond to these events. Whether we realize it or not, most of us carry around one or more irrational ideas that point us in an unbalanced direction. These may cause us to react more strongly and inappropriately to events than is warranted.

In his research, psychologist Albert Ellis put forth the idea that an emotionally healthy person accepts themselves as a valuable individual just because you are a human being. He also identified a number of common but irrational ideas. See if you recognize yourself in any of them:

- Adults must be loved by significant others for almost everything they do.
- Certain acts are awful or wicked, and the people who perform them should be damned.
- It's horrible when things are not the way we like them to be.

- Human misery is invariably caused by and forced on us by outside people and events.
- If something is or may be dangerous or fearsome, we should be terribly upset and obsess about it endlessly.
- It's easier to avoid than to face life's difficulties and responsibilities.
- We should be thoroughly competent, intelligent and achieving in all possible respects.
- Because something once strongly affected our life, it should indefinitely affect it.
- We always need something or someone stronger or smarter than ourselves to tell us what to do.
- We must have certain and perfect control over things.
- Human happiness can be achieved by inertia and inaction.
- We have virtually no control over our emotions and cannot avoid feeling disturbed about certain things.

All of these ideas are a bit crazy when you step back and think about them. In fact, it's not hard to visualize someone who is suffering from mental illness repeatedly thinking about several of them. We're fairly confident that the infamous Unabomber, Theodore Kaczynski, a man of undeniable intelligence (and someone who was technically trained but abhors the modern technical world) subscribes to some of these ideas.

We're not suggesting that if you've ever had one or two of these notions, that you are likely to turn into a psychopath or terrorist, but once you learn to recognize your irrational baggage, you can challenge those assumptions as they arise – and close the lid on them.

Some people have a more extreme form of self-limiting behavior known as obsessive-compulsive disorder, or OCD. While it's normal for most of us to occasionally check to see if we've locked our car, OCD sufferers can get trapped in an endless loop of negative behavior.

Mike once supervised a man who suffered from OCD. If he didn't take his medication (which happened from time to time), the poor fellow could take an hour to park his car in the company lot. He would drive into a parking spot, and then check all of the controls in the car. Next, he would get out of the car, walk around it, and check to make sure that all of the lights were off, the windows were closed, and so forth.

Inexplicably—unless you suffer from OCD or have a friend or family member that does—he would then open the front door, sit down in the driver's seat, and repeat the routine again and again. On some days, someone would have to go help him "break" his loop and coax him to work. Nevertheless, he was an excellent worker—as long as he could work in near isolation.

Slowly, neuroscientists are unlocking the brain chemistry that seems to drive OCD, but it seems clear that medication alone can't cure this malady. OCD victims need assistance from others, in the form of therapy, usually in conjunction with medication, to control their disease. However, one of the most difficult problems that OCD sufferers confront is a simple idea that seems both reasonable and rational: "My symptoms, while problematic, aren't really that bad. People around me can deal with it. I can't change right now - I don't want to upset anyone. I don't want people to think I'm becoming someone else."

You need to overcome that kind of irrational idea, the belief that improving your behavior will cause your friends to disappear, if you want to become a more productive Fourth Wave leader. If you want balance, and you want to do great things, you have to be able and willing to recognize when you fall into these irrational behaviors, and then to do new things that make these less likely in the future.

We all fall into one of these self-defeating patterns of behavior from time to time. Neither Rob nor Mike have ever met anyone who didn't—including each other. Engineers are maybe the most vulnerable of all professions in this regard. They've become conditioned to being seen as a bit eccentric or at least a bit different from everyone else, and they like it.

You can't let these weaknesses turn into an obsession. Like Robert Kearns, sensing and addressing an injustice or unfairness is fine—until it becomes a fixation.[1] Then, it becomes self-defeating and possibly self-destructive.

But that doesn't mean you are likely to suffer from OCD or be a sociopath just because you have some of these thoughts occasionally. On the other hand, you must try and develop enough self-reflection that you can face up to the inevitable failings we all have from time to time.

So, the time has come to set down those aspects of your behavior that you think are the most troubling and most likely to knock you out of balance—things we call "blind spots." Three is probably enough, and we'll provide you with plenty of ways to push these out of your life in the rest of the

---

[1] The story of Philo Farnsworth and his duel with David Sarnoff of RCA over the rights to color television is similar to Kearns' tale.

book. Again, there is a place for this on the "Step A-Forever" worksheet.

Pasick Personal Leadership Development Plan
Know Yourself--*Enduring Standards For Personal Behavior*
What Is Your Leadership Baseline?
E. What Blind Spots Do You Need To Watch? *(Self defeating patterns of behavior)*
1
2
3

Summing Up—Your Assignment

If you've read this chapter and thought about things, you will now have five lists that establish your *leadership baseline*:

1. Your five key strengths
2. A personal mission statement
3. A clear personal vision
4. Your five critical core values
5. Two or three of your self-defeating weaknesses or blind spots

If you haven't done so, now is the time to complete the "Step A-Forever" Worksheet in the Personal Leadership Development Plan. If you haven't written anything down yet, you should use the worksheet to create your "Forever" assessment.

These personal evaluations will set the stage for what we will discuss in the remaining chapters of the book. (Again, the spreadsheet for this worksheet can be downloaded from the homepage at **robpasick.com**.) We recommend you use this spreadsheet because your results will automatically be copied to you're the "Summary Plan" worksheet in the Personal Leadership Development Plan.)

Pasick Personal Leadership Development Plan
Know Yourself--*Enduring Standards For Personal Behavior*
What Is Your Leadership Baseline?

A. List your 5 Key Strengths *(What are the things you do best?)*
1.
2.
3.
4.
5.

B. What Is Your Mission *(What are you here on earth to do?)*

C. What Is Your Vision? *(Your future picture of success over the next 10 years)*

D. What Are Your Core Values? *(Guiding principles, even when the going gets tough)*
1.
2.
3.
4.
5.

E. What Blind Spots Do You Need To Watch? *(Self defeating patterns of behavior)*
1.
2.
3.

CHAPTER FOUR

Time to Get More Specific: Entering The Matrix

Now that you've developed the first portion of self-awareness—the positive side—it's time to turn our attention to the other side. Like Neo in *The Matrix* movie series, you need to free your mind from the limitations imposed by your previous experiences. To start, you need to complete a simple exercise we call *The Relationship Matrix*.

For any simple matrix, you need rows and columns. Create a column with six headings—or use the "Step-B Foundation Matrix" in the Personal Development Leadership workbook. These headings are You, Friends & Community, Career, Your Family, Your Health, and Your Integrity. Then, create six columns with the same six headings. If you are doing this without the workbook, it should look something like this:

Pasick Personal Leadership Development Plan
Understanding Your Surroundings
Who & what matters in your life?

	You	Friends & Community	Career	Your Family	Your Health	Your Integrity
You						
Friends & Community						
Career						
Your Family						
Your Health						
Your Integrity						

After you have constructed this basic matrix, you need to address the blank cells—the shaded cells are redundant. Each white cell is an *interaction* within your life. How do you relate to your community and friends—and how do your community and friends impact your health? All of the possible interactions can be described using the Relationship Matrix.

Now, with your mission, vision, values, strengths, and irrational weaknesses in mind, rate each of the interactions as follows:

- Strong—this interaction is powerful in my life
- Moderate—this interaction has some impact in my life
- Weak—this interaction doesn't affect my life much

After you've decided the strength of each interaction, now rate the impact of each interaction on your life:

- Positive (+)—my life is better because of this interaction
- Neutral (N)—my life is neither better nor worse as a result of this interaction
- Negative (-)—this interaction is causing me some difficulty or discomfort

When you've completed this, you will almost certainly see a pattern. There will be some areas that are strong and positive, others that are weak and less positive. We think that a well-balanced leader has no more than one or two cells that are weak, and almost none that are negative. Any cell that is negative or weak should certainly command your attention, because a that kind of interaction is likely to be a spot in your life that will, sooner or later, interfere with accomplishing your vision and advancing your mission.

Men and women tend to focus on different cells. For women, it's often the conflict between their roles as leaders in their career and as wives and mothers in their families. As Michelle Obama told an audience on the presidential campaign trail in 2008, her husband, Barack, "has seen me worry that when I'm at work, I'm not spending enough time with the kids. And when I'm with the kids, I'm not spending enough time at work. Never feeling like I'm doing anything right -- always feeling just a little guilty."

For men, a common problem is feeling as if they're not achieving enough at work. As one of Rob's clients put it, "No matter how hard I work, I never seem to be able to keep up. If I'm doing one thing, I'm constantly interrupted by my iPhone or a hundred other things that seem to grab my attention. The faster I go, the further behind I get. ... I fear this all will come crashing in on me someday. I know I should also be attending to my health, but I have no time to exercise or eat well."

Mike has personal experience with this kind of imbalance. He's always led a full-speed existence, starting and developing three companies over his career, raising two children, coaching youth travel ice hockey (which is almost a full-time job in itself) and playing both golf and hockey with gusto. (He took up hockey in his mid-thirties when his aging knees and ankles wouldn't permit him to play basketball, flag football, or softball.) His career work often caused him to travel, including significant international travel from time to time.

However, this was an unsustainable mix. Eventually, his health suffered. As a result of stress, physical exertion, some bad luck, and simple wear and tear, he has had one foot surgically screwed and pinned together, both hip joints replaced, and two stents implanted for severe arterial blockages in his heart. Then, while playing golf (of all things), he suffered a serious slip-and-fall accident and the result was a complicated fracture of his thigh bone. Significant surgery, three weeks in the hospital, and months of rehab followed.

He was back at work almost as soon as he was released from the hospital, though, and six months after he had recovered from his broken leg, Mike suffered a heart attack. A blood clot (which probably formed when he was bed-ridden from his broken leg) had become lodged in one of his arterial stents. He's fully recovered and healthier than he ever was even when he was quite active, but that sequence of events has made him utterly aware that balance is far more important than he ever realized.

Still, he was lucky. One of the arterial blockages was in a critical cardiac artery; he could have keeled over and died at any moment if the blockage had not been opened with a stent. His slip-and-fall accident could have been fatal had he landed on his head or neck instead of his leg.

If you really have the courage to complete the matrix honestly, you can quickly pinpoint areas where tension and stress are entering your life. When Mike completed the matrix after his heart attack, he found (not surprisingly) that the major negative influences revolve around his health. In particular, the pressure of his career had a strong and negative influence on his health. He came to realize that he wouldn't get many more chances and needed to change some of his behaviors.

So, your next step is to set five key goals that support your vision and create a brief action plan to achieve these goals (we'll explore that in the following chapters). No one is powerless to affect their future—if you think that, you've fallen into one of the irrational weaknesses we warned you about in the last chapter. If you clearly identify some goals and start acting on the plan, you are likely to feel better immediately.

But if you remain in denial and do nothing, chances are the deficit in accomplishment will eat away at you.

Now, let's discuss a few important issues that you should learn about now and keep in mind while setting your goals.

Set Goals You Can Achieve

Engineers are strange at times. Often, they are the world's greatest realists. Now and then, they're romantic dreamers, visualizing nearly (or actually) impossible feats. You simply can't afford to be unrealistic when setting personal goals, and that means there must be a practical expectation that you can accomplish something. You don't want to set a one-month goal of running in a marathon if you're unable to jog a mile without puffing and wheezing.

Moreover, goals are more specific and easier to measure than the details in your vision. A vision is a more complex summary of actions and accomplishments that further your mission, while goals are the bricks that turn your vision into reality.

Through the exercises we've suggested, we've actually been helping you develop a detailed "structure" for improving and developing your leadership skills. We think a simple diagram will show you what you've been doing up to this point.

Your Mission

Your Vision

| Goal 1 | Goal 2 | Goal 3 | Goal 4 | Goal 5 |

Daily Behaviors—Core Values

- Friends & Community
- Career
- Family
- Health
- Finances

The structure you've been building is, in the grand scope of things, all about pursuing the adventure, excitement, and, ultimately, the fun and enjoyment that's implicit in your mission. But to do that, you have to have a more exact, but still relatively general set of objectives, which you have captured in your vision statement.

Now, you need to break this down into more detailed achievements. To be a realist, you have to be specific. Your goals should be something measurable that you can have some probability of reaching. So focus on things that you can control. Realize, too, that you can't control someone else's behavior, though you can control your reaction to their behavior.

And, if you look at the diagram, you'll see that the goals you want to attain are supported by the daily behavior that you exhibit. Finally, you'll notice that your daily behavior sits atop the external factors that determine your balance points—the same issues that we just examined in creating your Relationship Matrix.

You can also learn about personal balance by looking at the stability of this structure. You might be able to make serious progress toward your vision if you have one or possibly two frail goals. But, if you have three goals that are either not well focused—or you aren't even close to achieving—the chances that you'll bring about your vision are not good. It might also be true that, if you are having difficulty with just one key goal (say Goal 1 or Goal 5 on the flank of the structure), your vision might still come crashing down.

That same situation is true for the five external factors from the Relationship Matrix. We've arranged the matrix so that the friends/community and integrity pillars are on the flank of the structure—if you have negative or weak interactions in these places, you could see the collapse of everything you are doing. But you might have trouble with your family—and, for a time, you might get away with something, just as Mike has been able to keep things going even though he short-changed his physical health for a number of years.

Sooner or later (and we all know Murphy's Law), the heavy weight of your daily behaviors, goals, vision and mission will cause the structure to sag and perhaps give way. You might choose to place a different external factor on the flank than we have, but we think you can see the principle we're suggesting.

Ultimately, you need to choose goals that can be stated in achievable steps. For example, one of your goals may be to quit smoking. But the first step might be to limit the number of cigarettes you smoke in a day. Then you might not allow yourself to smoke after your meals. A further step might be to deny yourself a smoke before 10 AM. Each step takes you closer to fulfilling an explicit goal, and finding things that you can get done in a reasonable period will bring you a sense of triumph and satisfaction—which, in turn, will drive you to the next achievable step.

And finally, when you attain one of your goals, enjoy your success. Reward yourself. Buy something you've wanted, or take a trip you've been meaning to take. Do something that brings a smile to your face. But—be careful. Sometimes, we reward ourselves in a way that brings out another negative interaction in your relationship matrix. That's one of the reasons why people who try to quit smoking often gain weight; they reward themselves with other oral satisfactions, and they just trade one weakness for another.

If you think about your reward in the context of your goals, that can make it all into a self-energized reaction. You do something that brings you joy—and you reward yourself with something that helps you reach the next delight. If you keep doing this, you'll find you don't have much opportunity to fall into the weaknesses or bad habits that you've built up over the years.

Commit to Action

We suggest a simple goal-setting method that Rob learned from a colleague many years ago. You can develop each of your goals using this outline:

- **What?** The specific, measurable goals that you want to achieve. No vague dreams, please. Record the date you're setting them.

- **By when?** The date by which you want to achieve the goals. Research shows that 90-day goals can be most effective. Longer-term ones tend to get lost in day-to-day activities; shorter-term ones come to resemble to-do lists.
- **Why?** The reason why each goal is important. What values are central to the goals?
- **How?** The process, step by step, that will you use to achieve each goal.
- **Support?** The people you will work with to achieve your goals.

Rob has been at this for a while. He keeps his own goals on index cards, and he has a box of them dating back to 1968. For Rob, index cards work because they fit his work habits. They remind him of the things he had decided are important. What do I want to do? How fast am I going to get it done? Why do I want to do it? How will I get it done? Who will help me? As a reminder of the goals he has set, Rob carries a folded-up index card in his wallet listing his goals. He updates this list as his life unfolds each day.

Your plan doesn't have to be extremely detailed, but you do need a plan to translate goals into action. Rob's low-tech version is simple and effective. And it's easily adaptable to our electronic world. The Personal Leadership Development Plan workbook described previously can help you do that. We'll discuss that in a moment, but we need to think a bit more about what will be needed to realize your goals.

Pick Your Support Team

One of the myths that people often hold dear is that they are responsible for their own success. Americans, in particular, have always believed in the power and splendor of a strong, gallant individual, whether it was John Wayne as a flying Marine, Sylvester Stallone as Rocky or Rambo, or Mark Hamel as Luke Skywalker.

But the popular fable of solo success has rarely been accurate. No one flies a fighter plane without dozens of support personnel. In fact, the importance of cooperation and support has been true throughout American history. On July 3, 1776, Ben Franklin told the Continental Congress—which was about to release the Declaration of Independence—"We must all hang together or assuredly we shall all hang separately."

This is a very telling statement. It's easy to forget that the men who signed this document were deeply engaged in a treasonous act against their own government, punishable by death. Worse, they had committed treason against the world's preeminent superpower of the 18th century, the British Empire. Had their insurgency failed, they would have been hunted down and most of them could well have met their fate on the gallows.

In the myth of strong individual accomplishment that Americans seem to love, it's even easier to forget that the revolution proclaimed in the Declaration came perilously close to failure again and again. One of the primary reasons for this was the inability of the Americans to "hang together."

Each state wanted control over their own militias, the Continental Congress repeatedly hamstrung Washington and the Continental Army with poor financial support—because the states were bickering over who would pay—and finally, petty jealousies and scrambles for power among Continental military leaders. The defection of Benedict Arnold, who didn't get the credit he felt he deserved for his heroics (and serious wounds) in the pivotal Battle of

Saratoga, then betrayed his comrades for what he hoped would be glory and honor in the British Empire, and could have destroyed the rebellion.

It may be hard for some Americans to accept this, but the reality is that the Americans would probably not have been able to force the British to surrender three years after Saratoga but for the assistance of the French navy. And—the assistance of the French came about largely because of Arnold's actions in securing a major victory over the British.

In early September of 1781, a French fleet attacked the British Navy in Chesapeake Bay. French Admiral de Grass proceeded to drive off the British Navy and then began bombarding British positions near Yorktown. As a result, the British ground forces were sandwiched between George Washington and his American army and the French navy. Soon, with food and ammunition nearly gone, the Continentals attacking on the ground and the French blocking the only path of escape, General Cornwallis and 8,000 British troops surrendered about 6 weeks after the French fleet arrived.

If, however, de Grass had not been present, Cornwallis would simply have boarded British ships and fled, probably back to New York. It's doubtful the Americans could have pursued an endgame for long against the determined wealth and power of the British Empire without the pivotal assistance of the French navy.

Even after the revolution was over, the newly independent United States floundered under a hopelessly weak national umbrella known as the "Articles of Confederation." The disunity that resulted was so disastrous that another insurgency, called Shay's Rebellion, soon frightened the powerful property owners in the states. They convened a new group, and the result was the American Constitution, a document that enshrined the common purposes of all of the 13 states in a way that has, with relatively modest changes, continued to this day.

But rugged, solitary individual achievement wasn't really a major element in this story.

In the past two decades, more and more people have realized that if you are going to succeed in a highly interconnected and complex world, it will be within a community, a group of other committed souls. Of course, technology—and technical organizations—have played a critical role in this shift. The success of LinkedIn, Facebook and other social media sites is changing society and careers in ways that no one really understands or can readily predict.

If you are willing to accept that most significant accomplishments arise through cooperation and pooling of effort, it's clear that you must think about who will support you and help fill in the gaps in your abilities and resources.

This takes on even greater importance during bad economic times. If you lose your job, your network might help you find a new one. Isolated people have a much harder time of it. And by networks, we don't mean just online communities. Your network might be your bowling league or an investment club or those who worship with you—anyone in the community or among your friends might be someone to call upon for collaboration, support, or other assistance.

Don't forget that families form another major pillar of the structure you are building, too. You don't need to have access to the Internet to call on parents, siblings, children or your partner for aid, support, or action.

You might want to hold a family roundtable to discuss what everyone thinks should be the family's mission, or vision, or values or house rules. Discuss the goals you are trying to achieve with your partner. Team building isn't something that you should leave behind when you shut the office door behind you.

It's Never as Easy as It Looks: Resiliency Counts

Another American myth is the idea that life should be a smooth progression of unending success. Once again, that's Hollywood fantasy. Real life is beset with struggle and often with repeated failure, even tragedy, before anything meaningful is accomplished.

Resilience is the ability to rebound from hardship, difficulty and misfortune and successfully adapt to adverse situations. Because the world is more interconnected than at any time in history, this is something that no one should ignore. As technology shrinks time and distance, and trade and cultural exchanges become the norm in the world, challenges seem more intense, grow more rapidly, and occur with greater frequency. The worldwide financial turmoil of 2008-2009 was a perfect example. The rise of deep-seated nationalism in many quarters is a harbinger of potentially dramatic change. And finally, the COVID-19 pandemic is almost certain to change many things in completely unpredictable ways.

Few events that are later seen as great in life are achieved without major risk and messiness. To deal with this, it's important to understand how you have handled adversity in the past. That's the best predictor of how you will handle it in the future. Almost everyone has bounced back from negative experiences at some point in their lives, but some people seem to be more resilient than others. What are the major factors that are present in highly resilient people?

Here's a summary of a dozen factors we think will predict your own resiliency. No one has all of these attributes, but those who regularly exhibit more than half of them usually respond to the downside of life more quickly and vibrantly than those who lack most of these behavioral patterns.

1. Carefully decide what you can control and what you can't. Focus on the things that you can affect, and don't fret about those you can't. You may need to watch and react to things that are outside of your control, but trying to change things that are beyond you is not only frustrating, it's a serious waste of energy, time, and often, of money.

2. Keep perspective on your ultimate goals; revisit your vision and mission statements frequently. Don't be afraid to alter these statements if events intervene, or if you decide something else is more important to you. (But be careful about doing this too often or just because you've hit a bump in the road!)

3. Be flexible; many people throughout history have suffered major losses, including their own lives, from being too rigidly attached to routines, methods, jobs—even their luggage!

4. Don't let short term gain seduce you into quitting, cheating, or exploiting others. Remember, you're unlikely to drift away from your values in large jumps, but rather in small, incremental, "who'd notice anyhow" steps.

5. Keep yourself inspired: read, discuss, pray; do whatever builds your spirit. Humor helps, particularly when you seem to be swimming upstream.

6. When things look darkest, remind yourself about how you got out of the last mess you were in!

7. Don't let pressure and longing for attractive possessions rob you of your health—while some stress is natural and even invigorating, unending pressure frequently leads to poor diet, lack of exercise, and even death. While the COVID-19 virus is a serious threat, how many will <u>not</u> succumb to the virus but be felled by stress, anxiety, and even panic?

8. Don't allow fear to control you. Remember, fear is a natural survival instinct, and a totally fearless person is usually a fool. Instead, find a way to tame it and make it work for you, just like a skater trying a difficult new stunt. Real courage means moving forward when you are too scared to move.

9. Commit to overcoming adversity – to win and not to allow yourself to fail. That means you need to make decisions and then go forward. When things do go wrong, don't hesitate to forgive yourself, particularly if you used sound logic and good information to make a decision. You're not perfect and you never will be.

10. It's important to be optimistic, but not Pollyannaish. Pessimists often become victims of their own predictions—"See, I told you that wouldn't work!" Taking foolish risks isn't wise, either.

11. Find a small group of people who are willing and able to support you. If someone is chronically negative, don't hesitate to move away from them.

12. Define specific and possible goals. And when things go badly, stick to the facts, no matter how bleak. Most people can accept bad news, but deception and unnecessary surprises drive everyone crazy.

When things seem to be going badly, pull out this list and read it. We think you'll find it helpful and useful—and that it will keep you from being sucked in by negativity. If you think things are bad and they can't get better, you'll probably have a self-fulfilling prophesy. On the other hand, if you can see how the tide can turn—and you actively pursue those actions—you're much more likely to start heading in the direction you'd rather go.

Your Goal Setting Assignment

You are now at the point where you should complete the "Step C-Strategic Goals" Worksheet. On this worksheet, you'll see where we've created space for you to list your high-level goals in the first column. We've also created columns where you can summarize the underlying structure of these goals, the when, why, how, and the support that's needed for these goals to be more than vague wishes.

Pasick Personal Leadership Development Plan
What Do You Want To Achieve *In The Next Three To Five Years?*
Do These Goals Support Your Mission and Vision?

	Date Goal Was Set	Target Completion Date	Why?	With whose support?
Strategic Goal No. 1				
Strategic Goal No. 2				
Strategic Goal No. 3				
Strategic Goal No. 4				
Strategic Goal No. 5				

A Resource for Balance: The Coach's Clipboard

If you've done all of the things we've suggested thus far, you are probably becoming aware that you need to develop new behaviors, while slowly crowding any irrational thoughts about the world off your personal agenda. You've also started to see that structured planning enables you to turn your ideas into action.

Of course, there's still a long journey ahead to turn goals into accomplishments. And, unless you are living a charmed life, there will be more than a few bumps in the road ahead. More than anything, you need to build more elements of the leadership skills that will make a difference.

As Mike and Rob both know from their experiences, you can have a great plan with plenty of details, but it will be the moment-by-moment acts you perform that will convert a strategic blueprint into reality. That requires personal strength and emotionally balanced leadership.

When the affairs of the world are out of balance, as they are with the COVID-19 pandemic raging, it's essential that you have your personal balance firmly established.

In the following chapters, you'll find a year's worth of leadership principles that can help you develop the daily behaviors you need to reach your goals, achieve your vision, and support your mission. Based on the factors we think lead to balanced leadership—which we identified in the introduction section—we've created a detailed list of behavioral guidelines that will help you become a more balanced and more influential leader, someone that others will start looking to you for guidance, assistance, and support. Collectively, we've called these five groups of behavior suggestions "The Coach's Clipboard" and each suggestion draws on real-life examples from our work and lives. There's one chapter for each principle.

Within each chapter, we've included suggested behaviors that support each category of behaviors. Matched to each principle is a short list of suggestions for specific actions we call "The Playbook," which includes discussion points and strategies you can use and adapt as you see fit. Not everyone will find each one of these things useful. Not everyone needs to address every one of these points. However, almost everyone will find several ideas that can help you build a structure of behavior that will support your quest for your goals, your vision, and your mission.

Our goal is to be inclusive and informative, to have some fun and, most of all, to offer advice that is practical and effective.

Ready?

CHAPTER FIVE

The Coach's Clipboard: Knowing Who You Are

If you are going to reach your goals, you need to know yourself. You can never have all of the answers because *no one* ever has all of the answers. And you can't do everything yourself even if you did have full knowledge about things you are working on at any moment.

More than that, you've got to come to grips with the fact that you can never hope to keep everything in balance at the same time. There will be days where work dominates your personal life, and days where personal crises make your career seem irrelevant. If you really hope to weather these dynamic shifts in personal fortune, you need to understand who you are.

We helped you get started with this in Chapters 3 and 4. Now, we can offer you some specific actions that you can use to improve your knowledge of who you are and what you can—and can't—do well.

Behavior 1. Think before you act.

People with a technical bent are often bubbling over with ideas. Despite the stereotype that many non-technical people have of engineers, they are often gregarious, outgoing, and argumentative—particularly when they are in the middle of a technical discussion with other tech heads.

If you observe meetings where engineers are discussing and evaluating ideas, insights, criticisms, and innovative concepts bounce around the room with much greater frequency than equations or other deductive patterns of thought.

Business consultant Robert Fritz advises in his book "The Path of Least Resistance," that you take time before you act to ask yourself a key question: What result do I wish to create?

When technical people find themselves deeply engrossed in a subject, they seem to act with a stream-of-consciousness that can be powerful as well as destructive. If the room you are in is full of people you know well, and they are all conversant with the subject at hand, a free-flow, stream-of-consciousness discussion can be a powerful and productive outcome.

On the other hand, if you are meeting with people from a variety of disciplines and backgrounds, as you might with a cross-functional team, you need to recognize that your actions can have a bigger impact than you imagined or intend. Sometimes actions bring the desired positive outcome; other times, they trigger unanticipated negative consequences.

How can you sort through things, particularly when the fur is flying in a meeting, and know what will work and what won't? Communication is a complex subject. Studies have shown that 60 to 90% of the actual information transmitted in an oral discussion is non-verbal, coming from your body language and facial expressions. (That's one of the reasons that most teleconferences are so dull and tedious.)

Whether you are in a small meeting, sending an email, or talking on the phone, communication often gives birth to new or modified ideas. When you interact with people, you work through a predictable pattern. It starts with identifying something that needs to be done: an improvement, a solution to a problem, or something completely new. This leads to one or more decisions about what to do, and then you need to create an action or a reaction. If you don't think about what you're saying ahead of time, you may trigger effects that you didn't intend.

In physics, there's an important concept called Heisenberg's Uncertainty Principle. While this rarely matters in large scale activity, it can be critical at the atomic level. This principle says that you really can't measure anything with compete precision, because the act of measuring changes what you are trying to measure.

To illustrate this, think about measuring the diameter of a floating soap bubble with a ruler. If you touch the ruler to the bubble, it may change shape or even burst. If you hold the ruler at a distance from the bubble, you will have trouble with parallax—if you move the ruler closer you will "measure" a bigger diameter, and if you move it away, you will perceive a small diameter on the ruler scale.

In business as well as life, we have the same problem, but it comes in a somewhat different form. Often called the Law of Unintended Consequences, this isn't a scientific law, but it is something that occurs so often that, like Murphy's Law, it's an idea we have to take seriously.

In a more elegant form, we can restate this law as follows: when you take an action, you are creating a cause. That leads to an effect, presumably the desired effect. However, because the world is complicated, we nearly always get more than the desired effect; we also get many unintentional effects as well. Most of these are so trivial we don't notice, but we also may cause an effect that's much bigger as well as being counter-productive.

In the world of pharmaceutical drugs, this is almost an article of faith. If there are no side effects from a drug, then it's unlikely there will be any central or therapeutic effect.

In particular, engineers tend to be too bold and impulsive when they are comfortable with the topic. They jump into something too quickly, but don't think about how someone with less knowledge might react to their idea.

THE PLAYBOOK

- As you work through a decision and actions, take the long view. Is this something that supports or matches your identified goals, vision and mission? See if you can associate a phrase or a few words that illustrate how these things work together.

- Think before you speak and don't allow the Reptilian complex in your brain to work its primal and powerful influence on the words that might follow.

- If you blurt things out in large meetings, practice speaking slowly in private. When Mike realized he had this problem, he would spend time, alone at home, "debating" with himself in front of a mirror. He realized his face started to show that he was about to react very pointedly before he was even certain what line of reasoning he was about to follow. He's gotten better at this, but instinct still wins over at times.

- Not speaking up can be equally negative. If you clearly see a difficulty with something being discussed in a meeting, and you don't say anything, you are postponing a likely problem. Try to offer at least a short outline of a possible solution—lest you be labeled a pessimistic critic. If you are going to a meeting where disagreements are likely, write down a few ideas about how you can make an idea you don't agree with into a plan that you can support—a plan of action that addresses the weakness you think could sink the project.

Behavior 2. Recognize your blind spots and bad habits.

When you are driving on a freeway, you can see notices on many large trucks that say, "If you can't see my mirrors, then I can't see you." What does this mean? In a sermon at the Westminster Presbyterian Church in Buffalo, John Gilbert Horn made a wonderful observation about these notices: "Well, at least the driver knows where his blind spots are, even if he doesn't know who or what is in them." Blind spots arise when we look at the wrong things or look in the wrong way, often because we are overloaded with other information, preconceptions or even prejudice.

In some cases, a blind spot might turn into a bad habit that you don't recognize—like not paying attention when you are passing a large truck.

To start digging into your blind spots and bad habits, ask yourself these questions:

- Are you a perfectionist who can never admit that you, *like everyone*, has flaws and—at times—one or more of the irrational thoughts we described in Chapter 3?
- Do you find that you just can't ignore your email even when you are facing a deadline?
- Are you so eager to get your way that you would distort facts, intimidate people, and otherwise behave in ways that might cause others to distrust you?

Mike has carried out an exercise with engineering managers and supervisors for years. He asks them to list of the five most common management errors they have seen in their careers. There are many answers, but one answer comes up every time: micromanagement. It might not be number one on every list, and it might be called something else, but it is always on each list. Engineers-as-managers seem to fall into this as a default-mode of operation more than any other group.

Why does this happen? Most first-time managers find that one or two of their team members let them down at some point. Add to this the likelihood most new technical supervisors tend toward perfectionism, and you have the perfect recipe for micromanagement. It's so common in technically-driven organizations that it makes you wonder how people can do something over and over again that so many people dislike.

First-time managers are often oblivious to what follows. They say to themselves, "I trusted this person; they let me down. I won't let that happen again; I'll make sure my reports do exactly what they need to do, and if they don't, I'll show them how to do it by doing it myself." Before they realize it, this becomes their basic roadmap for managing others. Do they realize this? Rarely—and this bad habit/blind spot that results probably causes as much employee dissatisfaction, particularly in technical organizations, as any other managerial behavior.

THE PLAYBOOK

- Poll people who have known you for a long time and ask them to help you identify your bad habits. You might buy them lunch to get the discussion going— but just listen and don't get defensive when they tell you what they can see that you can't!

- When things don't go the way you want, think about self-defeating behaviors (like micromanagement) that can be triggered by blind spots. Don't worry that you haven't been perfect in the past and don't flog yourself because you aren't perfect.

- Remember, you can't please everyone all of the time. If you try, you will fail. In fact, if you aren't willing to constructively confront someone who disagrees with you, you aren't ever going to be very influential—which means you won't be a leader.

Behavior 3. Know your emotional IQ.

Technical people often realize they are different when they are growing up. They were "brains" and got the good grades, in many cases with less effort than their classmates. The most driven of these adolescents can be obnoxious and overbearing, too. They've got high traditional IQs, but often their emotional IQs lag far behind. When they become adults, these characteristics frequently carry over to their work and personal life.

If you're going to have emotional smarts as well as traditional intelligence, you must become more aware of your own feelings. You also need to develop an ability to read the emotions of other people, to remain calm when things are crazy, and—as a leader, manage the emotions of work groups.

In the technical arena, most of the work eventually involves managing a team or a meeting. It's a bit like being an orchestra conductor – sensing how the group is feeling, knowing when to call on someone, recognizing who hasn't been participating. This takes patience and a clear recognition that not everyone can think as fast as you can; you need to let things develop.

However, the traditional orchestra conductor is one of the last all-powerful dictators, the last upholder of absolute authority in western civilization. In their book *Leadership Ensemble*, Harvey Seifter and Peter Economy describe the world-famous Orpheus Chamber Orchestra, which has no conductor. They rehearse, perform, and even record without the traditional baton-wielding maestro indicating the beat, emphasis, and movement of the music.

How do they do this? They bring this about by each member of the orchestra exhibiting leadership on a continual basis. In fact, Seifter and Economy suggest that there's actually much more leadership at work at Orpheus than in any other musical assembly, but this takes a great deal of emotional energy from every player and every section in the orchestra. Each section must plan how they will perform every movement, and then learn to coordinate and collaborate with all of the other sections. But they cannot simply sit in their chair and wait to be told what to do by a dictatorial conductor.

THE PLAYBOOK

- When someone causes you to erupt, remember that negative reinforcement is a blunt instrument, and your sharp critique is almost certain to cause other problems. Try and record the events that triggered your response. Was your credibility attacked? Was your honesty questioned? Did someone bring up an old grievance that caught you off-guard?

- When you hear something you don't agree with, try to find parts of the discussion that are praiseworthy and offer a sincere compliment. If there's something in the situation that you really can't abide, always start by asking the other person to clarify the idea. In many cases, you'll find you misunderstood what was actually expressed. In other cases, you'll find the other party talking themselves out of their position.

> In the end, if you really understand their position and you still can't support their view, you can offer some respectful disagreement rather than a biting criticism.
>
> - If you walk away from a dispute and still feel unhappy, try writing a narrative of the disagreement from the other person's standpoint. We're amazed at how vicious the "comment" section is on the Internet. Most people believe this occurs because you can say terrible things about almost anyone when you can hide behind anonymity. Work, family, and community don't operate that way. You will need to work with someone you disagree with again in the future. If you verbally blast them, make sure you realize that this won't be forgotten or forgiven for a long, long time.

Behavior 4. Learn from your mistakes.

It's really quite simple. In the convoluted and dynamic world of technology, if you aren't learning you are falling behind. This means any and all forms of media are necessary resources for anyone who wants to be productive as a technologist.

In the complexity you face every day, errors and mistakes are inevitable. No one knows enough to get it right every time, every day. However, when you find you've made a mistake, ask yourself a simple question: have I done something like this before?

One of Mike's mentors, Dr. Howard B. Aaron, who was tragically killed in an auto accident many years ago, often told him, "Look, I know you're going to screw up. But at least be creative. Don't make the same mistake over and over again."

It's OK to be ignorant. No single person knows everything. However, once you've made a mistake, you can't claim to be ignorant the next time. If you make the same kind of mistake several times, you might really be stupid.

And stupid tends to be forever!

When companies or governments stop the learning process, alarm bells should go off, because that is when rigidity sets in, and failing to change and adapt in today's fast-paced world can be fatal. But both Rob and Mike see too many organizations that make the same mistake over and over again. Don't let this happen to you.

THE PLAYBOOK

- Join a business-related discussion group at work or through networking sites. Better yet, write reviews yourself! Once again, writing forces you to develop a greater understanding about what you know.

- Turn your company into a learning organization. Create a lessons-learned wiki or "things gone wrong" common folder in your company network. This is one of the great strengths of Toyota in the auto industry: they learn from each negative episode, and they do it without recrimination, finger-pointing, or loss of prestige for those associated with the original problem.

- Be careful, though, about previous mistakes; one of the worst things that you can ever say is "we tried that before and it didn't work." The situation might be different, new facts or new technology might be available, and what was wrong two years ago might be the best thing possible today.

Behavior 5. Know your limits.

If you know your limits – your strengths as well as your challenges – you'll spend less time trying to be something you aren't and do things that aren't likely to succeed. We tend to overvalue things we're not good at and undervalue what comes naturally.

When Mike was running a manufacturing company, his partner, Alex Bireescu, managed the operation of the factory. Mike handled other things, including engineering functions, R&D, sales and marketing, and accounting, administration, and finance. Mike realized the quality of their products, while better than average, still often failed to meet some of their customers' high expectations, particularly because they were concentrating on military and aerospace markets.

Mike tried to get Alex to accompany him on trips to visit demanding customers, but Alex always demurred, suggesting that he was too busy. He eventually admitted he never wanted to go because he didn't think he could be successful in these visits.

When Mike and Alex parted company and sold their interests in the business, Mike went on to consulting work while Alex started a new business similar to the one he and Mike had built. Mike stayed in touch with Alex, and even did some consulting for him.

Eventually, Alex, who had a strong personal will, forced himself to do what he didn't want to do—have more face-to-face interactions with customers. He found that he developed a high level of skill in this area—he still didn't enjoy it most of the time—but it helped him build a healthy business that he passed on to his son John when Alex succumbed to cancer a several years ago. Mike kept in touch with Alex almost to the end of his life, and Alex was clear about the importance of developing a skill he didn't think he could ever have.

The lesson is clear: to overcome your personal weak spots, you need to understand what they are.

THE PLAYBOOK

- Look back at your past failures and analyze what the components were. Where did you exceed your limits? Can you do something about this?
- Decide how much time you can devote to work each week before feeling burned out. List all of the things you need to do in the next week and separate them into two categories: those that will be disastrous if they aren't completed, and those that won't. Start with and concentrate on the do-or-die stuff first and see how much of your time remains when this work is complete. In times of crisis, someone needs to set priorities that are aligned with reality. If you can't do it all, at least take control and decide which things you will fail at! It's dead certain that if you try and do everything, you are much more likely to fail at every task on your list.
- Make a similar commitment to the hours you will spend with your family. Don't short-change them in favor of your job on a permanent basis. However, if a critical situation arises at work, almost every family will understand if you need to temporarily shift the balance. On the other hand, don't let the thrill and excitement of these critical episodes turn you into an adrenaline-junkie. If you do, you'll find you squeeze

- those you love right off your calendar, because you will start to think that every crisis, every issue is an end-of-the-world situation.
- Understand that you can never be all things to all people all of the time, but if you budget your energy wisely, you can more often provide the right thing for the right people at the right time. As Keith Richards and Mick Jagger wrote and sang,

  > *You can't always get what you want*
  > *But if you try sometimes you just might find*
  > *You get what you need*

- The COVID-19 pandemic has offered everyone a chance to learn this lesson. You can't control the behavior of others. You can only control your behavior. Even if something occurs outside of your control, you can only manage what you do in response.

Behavior 6. Practice self-control through physical discipline.

Meditation produces beneficial effects for the heart, brain and metabolic system, according to research done at Harvard Medical School. Physical exercise can have a similar effect. A short walk of 10-15 minutes or so can help you clear your mind. You can also use walking time to think through the next activity that's ahead.

If your life is so hectic you can't find time to do this, consider walking during your lunch hour. If you habitually eat lunch at your desk, you may need to rethink your priorities—are you really so busy you can't take a short break or share a meal with someone?

THE PLAYBOOK

- Set aside time for activities that will help you bring your mind and body under control, particularly when stress is high. What works for you might not be the same for others, but meditation, writing, prayer, walking, running, or simply sitting on a bench in the sun can create the calm you need to balance tasks and relationship in your life.

- Turn to a 12-step program if you need help with addiction problems. Very few people are able to address addiction without a strong social network, and self-help organizations really can be effective as long as you commit to the program. There are more than 200 of these groups worldwide, and if you have an addiction or an obsession that you can't control, you need to look to others for assistance. In some cases, turning to a qualified therapist may be valuable.

- Use drive time for reflection. Turn off your cell phone while driving and think. We've known for many years about the impact of cell phone usage on driving, as David Strayer at the University of Utah explained. "If you put a 20-year-old driver behind the wheel with a cell phone, their reaction times are the same as a 70-year-old driver who is not using a cell phone. It's like instantly aging a large number of drivers."

Behavior 7. If you're stuck, get unstuck.

The financial crisis of 2008-2009 put many organizations between a rock and a hard place. The COVID-19 pandemic of 2020 is once again creating these near-panic conditions. Businesses are tightly constrained because sales and revenue have declined or even crashed, yet they have to spend money to make money at some future point.

It's a bit like a subsistence farmer who finds he's had a bad harvest one year. He doesn't get sufficient yield to store enough food for the winter, and, by early March, the only food he has are the seeds he needs to plant as soon as the weather allows.

Should he eat the seeds? Or will he try to manage a semi-starvation diet that may deprive him of the strength to plant and harvest during the growing season?

Are you caught in such a dilemma? If you accept that you are trapped by circumstances beyond your control, you will find that this is again a self-fulfilling prophecy. You need to go into an out-of-balance condition for at least some period of time to avoid these traps, but you need clear assessments and take risks to escape.

As the 2008-2009 financial crisis was unfolding, Mike was discussing this with a 48-year-old engineer who was summarily let go from his automotive job. He was skilled, knowledgeable and hardworking, but his employer, facing economic disaster—lopped off 25% of their staff. Unlike previous reductions in force, most of those now without a job were top-level performers and weren't pink-slipped to simply clean out deadwood.

It was a near certainty that none of the engineers in this man's position would be able to find work in the area. And, it was equally clear that no one with a family was likely to be able to sell a house in the area anytime in the near future. Virtually every one of these people seemed to realize that, but they were reluctant to draw hard conclusions from their situations.

As difficult as it may be, Mike suggested that the engineer might have to temporarily relocate to another part of the country, find another job and live in a low-cost rental flat, and then see if he could sell his house and relocate his family if and when things change.

That would be a tremendous imbalance between career and family, but it would at least have the potential that balance could be restored at some point in the near future.

Two months later, this man was still unemployed and still living in suburban Detroit. He was, in effect, eating his seed corn. In subsistence farming, when trapped in a no-win dilemma, a farmer who does that is soon forced to abandon his farm and go somewhere else. He might even end up as a beggar or an indentured servant in some societies. However, he will likely die of starvation if he is adamant about hoping that good fortune will somehow rain down from above. He might die if he abandons the farm, but he is almost certain to starve if he stays and passively waits for assistance.

Few of us face such a draconian choice in life, no matter how bad things look. However, nearly everyone faces difficult decisions at some point, and it's so easy, so seductive to simply sit still and hope that things will get better. That might happen, but that kind of outcome is far less probable than the situation getting worse.

If you do just sit there, you are stuck. If you stay stuck, you might still prevail. But what are your chances? 1 in 5? 1 in 10? One in a million? You really need to ask yourself a very tough and honest question: if you are likely to fail, do you want to let others dictate the terms, or will you at least take control and decide the terms on which you *might* fail—and on which you might actually avoid failure?

THE PLAYBOOK

- If you find that you aren't cut out for a certain task or job, don't be afraid to ask to be reassigned. You may end up in a better place. If that doesn't work, you should not be afraid of starting a discreet but structured search for a new position somewhere else.

- When it comes to health issues, don't throw up excuses. If you know you must make a big change or face the possibility of illness or even death, you need to get over that as quickly as possible and start changing your behavior. In 2008, a cardiologist told Mike he needed a cardiac stent immediately. He told Mike he shouldn't go home, or even try to walk to the parking lot; he could drop dead at any moment. Mike, who had no history of heart problems and only modest symptoms, was understandably stunned. He found himself passing through denial, anger and bargaining in seconds but anything less could have been disastrous. He got unstuck and was lying on a gurney in minutes.

- Don't avoid something you really need to do because it isn't in your comfort zone. In fact, if you are stuck in a serious situation, you almost certainly need to do something you'd prefer not to do. After Mike's angioplasty was completed, he revised his diet and became more conscientious about exercise and his blood pressure. He constantly reworks and follows his plan, and his heart health improved measurably. His latest exam could no detect evidence of his heart attack. Like a novice skydiver, you have to jump out of the plane and trust your chute to open. You have to be ready to deploy the reserve, though. You can have a plan B, plan C or even, as one of Rob's friends says, "I'm up to plan M."

- In a time of strict limitations on social gatherings, work and free movement—the kinds of limits that the COVID-19 pandemic imposed—think about how you can use time that was previous used for new and useful ends. Is it time to reach out to old friends on social media? Is learning more about an important subject possible on-line? If you are home with your family, can you play games that are both fun and intellectually stimulating? Can you exercise more? In some ways, these periods have provided a gift of time, a gift that will evaporate unless you are clear-headed even in times of extreme uncertainty.

Behavior 8. Help yourself by helping those around you.

We've all heard this before: if life gives you lemons, then you need to make lemonade. Of course, that assumes you've got enough sugar to make lemonade, but the principle is the same.

Whenever you make decisions or do something significant, the odds are that it will have an impact on other people that are important in your career and in your life.

Most of us are sensitive to how we affect our immediate family, but it's easy to forget that other decisions you make can affect the world around you—in ways that lead to consequences in your day to day activities.

All of the things you can do in this area have an added benefit: they have a strong tendency to make you feel good inside. They're not necessarily things that others will see, but they are things that you will know about. And, when you feel good, your attitude becomes more positive. A positive attitude is *always* helpful in extending your influence with others. Grouchy, negative people just don't last long in leadership positions.

Happy people who offer encouragement are often those who are most productive and able to exert the most influence. As the late sales guru Zig Ziglar often said, "There has never been a statue erected to honor a critic."

THE PLAYBOOK

- Re-examine your personal finances regularly. Beyond meeting your risk-return goals, see if you can shape your investments by backing firms that make your job possible.
- Buy branded items from companies you work with frequently. When you do that, you're feeding the hand that feeds you instead of biting it.
- Twice a year, clean out your closets, your basement, your garage, or your storage lockers. Donate items to a cause you support. Not only will you have the satisfaction of helping others, you can gain a tax deduction as well. Beyond that, you'll create a neater, more open area for living—and that, too, will lead to a brighter, more positive manner that will be reflected in your day to day demeanor.

Behavior 9. Stop trying to control people.

Thinking that you can control the way other people behave is a delusion. It's difficult enough to control what <u>you</u> do every day and thinking that you can dictate to others may quickly turn you into a dreaded micromanager. As Rob often tells people he coaches, it's a losing proposition to try to control the activities of people around you. Learn to appreciate them instead.

And, if you can't appreciate what they do, try (to the degree possible) to ignore them. If you don't, you are allowing them to infect you with behavior you don't find appealing. Road rage is like that. You get cut off in traffic, so you decide to tailgate the other driver for the next three miles. Yes, you're sending a message, but you are also creating a danger for other people and putting your own vehicle and possibly your own life at risk.

Not even the President of the United States—quite probably the single most powerful person in the world—has control over everything. Don't think you can dominate your small corner of the world. You can influence events—after all, that's the essence of leadership—but you if you try to make everything and everyone behave the way you want, you are going to be extremely disappointed. And you won't be able to say that you are self-aware; instead, you'll be living in a world of self-deception and utter frustration.

THE PLAYBOOK

- No matter what your job is or what you're responsible for, treat everyone with respect. You can't expect to influence people if you act in a condescending manner. Contempt is like a rubber ball—it comes bouncing back to you.

- Be willing to concede that mood and behavior swings are normal behavior. No matter how well you know somebody, they'll have good days and bad days. Accept that life isn't always predictable instead of reacting as if each snit or fit is a sign of irrationality or resistance. Your good mood might be more contagious than their bad mood. Remember, Mr. Spock and Vulcans are pure fiction!

- When you work within a team, you can exert control over the way things are done with consistent and repeatable process outlines and procedures. Never forget, though, that the final outcome in any process will often be affected by things you can't directly manage. When things spin out of control, try and see where something unexpected entered into the situation—and create a plan to either prevent or minimize the damage the next time around.

Behavior 10. Apologize when you're wrong.

If you really want to be a leader, you must come to grips with a simple fact. Leading means getting out in front, where uncertainty is real and often poses danger. Being a leader also means acting before all of the facts and information are available.

Waiting (and waiting and waiting) until the picture of the future is clear usually means that you are now reacting to something that's already happened. It's no longer the future, and you'll see that you've become more of a follower than a leader.

All of this means that, without any doubt, you are going to make mistakes. As Alexander Pope famously wrote, "To err is human, to forgive is divine." By admitting to your blunders, you remind people that you share a common and human bond.

Engineers may be as vulnerable to the "never let 'em know you goofed" mentality as any profession. Trained in a discipline in which there are calculable and precise answers for problems, driven by the unerring laws of physics, engineers often mature with a deep seated belief that someday, when they are older and more experienced, they won't make any more mistakes. Nonsense!

Mike was infected with this notion in his earlier days, but eventually realized that the only way to avoid mistakes was to do nothing—and even then, sitting pat is often the wrong thing to do, too. Theodore Roosevelt, in 1910, after serving as the 26th US President, said it best,

> *"It is not the critic who counts: not the man who points out how the strong man stumbles or where the doer of deeds could have done better. The credit belongs to the man who is actually in the arena, whose face is marred by dust and sweat and blood, who strives valiantly, who errs and comes up short again and again, because there is no effort without error or shortcoming, but who knows the great enthusiasms, the great devotions, who spends himself for a worthy cause; who, at the best, knows, in the end, the triumph of high achievement, and who, at the worst, if he fails, at least he fails while daring greatly, so that his place shall never be with those cold and timid souls who knew neither victory nor defeat."*

THE PLAYBOOK

- Just because an equation gave you a number doesn't mean that you used the correct equation.
- Leaders aren't more perfect than other people. Be strong enough to admit a mistake and set the record straight.
- Hiding or ignoring your less-than-perfect traits is an even greater weakness. By admitting that he had

heart disease, Mike was able to do something about it. At first he felt ashamed to reveal that he wasn't invulnerable to poor diet, crazy schedules and long hours. He eventually found disclosing his problem didn't diminish other's view of him; instead, it made people more likely to open up about their own vulnerabilities as well.

- Recognize when you are being domineering. Make notes about the events that led you to this behavior, and when you fail, talk it out with the other guy—the sooner, the better.

- Apologize without adding blame. "I apologize ... but you started it" isn't much of an apology. It's not too far removed from childhood "are too—am not" arguments.

Behavior 11. Lighten up.

Bill, who works for one of Rob's clients, was going to have hip replacement surgery. He'd been in a lot of pain and was nervous about the operation. But his co-workers weren't about to let him go out the door without having some fun. They donned masks and latex gloves and wheeled in a make-believe hospital cart as if to prep him for surgery. There were lots of jokes and a special recovery kit. Everyone was in on it and gathered around to have a laugh and wish Bill well. It relieved everyone's tension.

Knowing how to laugh is important. In fact, Mike has had *both* of his hips replaced—and he's learned that making fun of himself is yet another way to connect with people and let them know that he's human. Since his consulting work often led him into situations where people and processes have gone badly (occasionally terribly) wrong, he's found that he can reduce tension and improve his effectiveness by laughing about his own problems.

Most folks really appreciate a leader who can laugh at himself. If you act like you'll never make a mistake, you'll be setting yourself up for a fall. When you make a mistake—and you will, sooner or later—everyone will make sure to rub your nose in it. There's a fine line, though, between being willing to laugh at yourself and acting like a buffoon. Humor is powerful, but engineers are notorious poor comics.

Here are some engineer-based jabs that we like, but may make many people groan:

> The world does revolve around me. I picked the coordinate system, I should know.
>
> An optimist thinks the glass is half full, the pessimist thinks it's half-empty. An engineer knows that the capacity of the container has been over-designed by a factor of approximately 1.905 assuming a 5% volume for the sloshing safety factor.
>
> Two antennas got married - the wedding was lousy, but the reception was outstanding.

THE PLAYBOOK

- As a leader, you set the tone. If you can laugh, your associates will be more than happy to laugh with you. However, when all you can see or talk about is the downside of something, that attitude is contagious, too.
- If you squelch play at work, you risk stifling creativity. Adults think fun is for children, but the reality is that kids often have the most imaginative minds on the

planet. Technical people can't resist an exciting mystery—see if you can find a way to make work exciting.

- Give yourself permission to play a bit each day. If you keep a to-do list, see if you can make one of the items into an entertaining task—and, if appropriate, try and involve someone else when you do.

- Be positive; say "yes" as often as possible. Too often, leaders think their job is to say "no" and to prevent anyone from taking risks. If you fall into this trap, you will soon become a micromanager, and you will lose influence with most of those you work with.

CHAPTER SIX

The Coach's Clipboard: Demonstrating Self-Control

If you now have a good understanding of who you are, you are ready to address some of the fine points in your behavior. Becoming a better leader that means you have to develop and practice greater control over your actions. You can't let your inner-alligator take charge very often, or people will lose confidence in your ability as a leader; your influence will decline, and you won't sway those around you on important issues.

But changing the way you behave isn't easy. To gain conscious and constructive control, you will have to concentrate and practice the calm and discerning manner that oozes from the kind of people who seem to be the most effective leaders in the first two decades of the 21st century.

Today, it really seems that most folks want to associate themselves with leaders who appear to be in balance—yes, they are passionate and driven—but these people always look like they've found a way to keep all of the crazy, unbalanced things around them from upsetting their equilibrium. Our observations, though, show that most of the most effective leaders are like ducks—calm and poised where you can see them, but paddling like crazy beneath the surface.

Behavior 1. Keep tweaking your life.

In technical organizations, the unexpected is truly becoming commonplace. If "the only constant is change," then change is here to stay. However, the changes we experience, whether we face dramatic technology shifts or tremors in the financial world, are never going to follow a predictable and orderly pattern.

If you manage to figure out what the future will bring when things change, you'll be rich and famous. (Full disclosure: neither Mike nor Rob is very rich or very famous...)

Even when a major disruption is predicted—as Bill Gates and many others predicted that a coronavirus pandemic was nearly inevitable—it's unlikely that the business world will mobilize until a crisis actually arises.

What does that mean? Well, to start with, you can't get overly comfortable with anything you are doing. One of the classic questions that human resource professionals like to ask a young applicant is "Where do you see yourself in five years?" While this probably won't get you the job you are interviewing for, a better retort might be another question, "Wow—does that mean you might offer me a five year no-layoff contract?"

The real point is that almost no one can see five years into the future. You should have a plan, yes—but as Dwight Eisenhower said, "Plans are nothing—planning is everything." What does this really mean? We think it means you should be forward looking, but always prepared to make changes in your plans to fit the way the world keeps changing.

The latest crisis—the COVID-19 pandemic—is ample evidence that dramatic and sudden change can happen at any time. Leaders know how to adapt, how to plan, and are sufficiently balanced to deal with these kinds of earth-shaking situations. Those that can't do these things are facing a difficult and mentally turbulent future and may not be able to cope.

As things change, what are you doing to continually re-center your career and your life? Do you need additional training, formal education, or wider experience? Are you simply waiting for these things to come to you, or are you actively engaged in seeking out what you might need to further your mission by reaching your goals and fulfilling your vision?

You can think of this like planning and then driving somewhere. You can use a GPS system to lay out the trip, and then you'll follow this plan. Once you're on the road, though, you'll have to make decisions about what lane to be in, when to stop for gas, and when and where to stop and eat. You might even find that local conditions, like a sudden storm, an accident, or some other event will cause you to change your plan.

So it is in any career and in life. You've got to be ready to change the details of your plans—to tweak them regularly—or you might find that the best laid plans often go off-course. If you're not prepared to adjust as the world around you changes, you can't maintain balance between tasks and relationships.

THE PLAYBOOK

- Whether you use an on-line tool or keep a pen-and-paper planner, review what you've done at the end of every quarter. You'll probably be surprised at the overall picture you see when you look. If you're happy with what you've done and where you've been, keep doing it. But we're willing to bet that that a quarterly calendar review will cause you to want to tweak your plan for the next quarter.
- If you feel that your latest assignments aren't getting you where you want to be, you may want to sit down

with your boss and discuss it. But don't go into this discussion without a plan; you shouldn't expect your supervisor to act as a career counselor. Develop a brief, written set of ideas or even specific plans that you have in mind.

- Throughout your life, you'll have to adapt to sustain your health. Don't neglect to factor these important moves into your schedule. As part of a quarterly calendar review, check and see if you left sufficient space for exercise, appointments with health professionals, and proper rest.

- On balance, your personal center of gravity is all about your values. Step back and look at your last quarter and see if you've found yourself going outside the lines with respect to the core values you believe in. Discuss this with the most important people in your life if you see conflicts you can't seem to resolve.

Behavior 2. Inspire, don't intimidate.

Some leaders achieve success by intimidation. It may work for a while, but like any dictatorship, it's not sustainable. You can't just look at results; you have to look below the surface.

Once a child reaches the age of 2 or 3, it's difficult to force that child to do something that he or she doesn't want to do. If you try and force them to eat strained peas, every parent knows that the peas are coming right back out, and soon.

It's the same at work. You need an approach that inspires good work, not dictates it. One of the hardest things for any leader to do is to maintain balance between consistent, process-driven work assignments and individual initiative.

Young start-up companies are often organic—they have few rules, and those rules are often ignored. Employees have substantial freedom in their work. This can work for a while, but if a start-up starts to grow and doesn't change this, chaos results.

As companies grow, they are more likely to become autocratic. There may be rules, but senior management disregards them as they see fit, and employees are seen as the major cause of problems. "Who screwed up this time?" is something you frequently hear. These kinds of businesses are vulnerable to executive whim; if the boss gets it wrong, the whole company, like lemmings, stampedes over the edge.

At some point, leaders in an organic or autocratic firm try to build rules to address these issues. The problem is that the resulting bureaucracy becomes a tyranny of mammoth proportion. "We can't do that, it's against Policy 1-237-44C." Rigid enforcement of rules, with significant negative reinforcement, usually follows whenever rules are bypassed or flaunted. This leads to a stunted, inflexible organization, and the end result can be failure on a massive scale.

In his book, *My Years with General Motors*, Alfred Sloan slowly but surely explains how GM grew out of a collection of companies, some organic and some autocratic, that was assembled by William Durant. A major crisis just after World War I left GM on the edge of dissolution, and the company turned to Sloan for salvation.

Sloan built the world's most efficient and effective bureaucracy in the 1920's and 1930's as a response to this. And, after World War II, with the US having the most powerful manufacturing base on earth, GM became an economic behemoth of unprecedented size and power. But trouble was already on the horizon.

As the world changed and slowly became more global, GM saw its power and glory slowly dissipate, until, in early 2009, it again teetered on the edge of complete collapse. While the details of this story will be studied for decades, one thing is clear: Sloan's original rules and formalities turned into a rigid, reinforced bunker that leaders hid in, hoping to avoid punishment for taking initiative, lest their initiative go off track. Even when original ideas sprung up, they were quickly ground down by the maze of rules and infighting that such rules spawn.[2]

What's the alternative? Should the rules just be discarded and an organic approach adopted? Almost no organization of any size or complexity can be led that way. There must be yet another way toward enduring success for an organization.

Leaders need to build an *enabling bureaucracy*—a place where the rules support employee tasks and employees, within reasonable but flexible limits, and have substantial control over their day-to-day work. In such an organization, the hierarchy drives learning to improve the business, and leaders become organizers, process managers, and teachers more than dictators or micromanagers.

To sum up, a leader can set an agenda that is either coercive or supportive. At the same, a system of rules (or lack of rules) is needed for any organization. Young businesses almost always start with almost no rules. Depending on the leadership, these businesses can be on a continuum from dictatorial—an *autocratic* structure—or broadly democratic—an *organic* structure.

---

[2] The bulk of the evidence suggests that, under Mary Barra, General Motors has set a new and more enlightened course over the period since the 2008-2009 bankruptcy. While it's difficult to know the day-to-day details, by all public accounts, Barra's performance generally fits the model of balance we have put forth.

Over time, if the business grows, rules are needed and usually proliferate. If the rules are enforced by coercive social pressure, a *coercive bureaucracy* may result. The companies tend to be inflexible and are vulnerable to deft competitors and don't respond well to rapid change—much like General Motors prior to bankruptcy.

If, through serious and persistent effort, leaders can sustain a supportive social environment, a company might evolve into an *enabling bureaucracy*. It's difficult to maintain, though, as there are always pressures to fall into intimidation or to loosen the rules and structure too much.

Nevertheless, dynamic organizations that have sustained success tend to have encouraging cultures and a workable yet flexible set of procedures and policies that everyone can follow.

Here's a graphic that illustrates the various alternatives that leadership can shape:

		Social Structure	
		Coercive	**Supportive**
Technical Structure	**Tight Bureaucracy**	**Coercive Bureaucracy** • Extensive, Detailed Rules • Rigid Enforcement With Negative Reinforcement • Hierarchical Control	**Enabling Bureaucracy** • *Rules Support Employee Tasks* • *Employees Have Substantial Control Over Work* • *Hierarchy Drives Learning To Reduce Mistakes*
	Loose Bureaucracy	**Autocratic** • Minimum of Rules or Rules Ignored By Leaders • Top-Down Hierarchical Control • Employees Seen As Major Root Cause of Problems	**Organic** • Minimum of Rules or Rules Ignored • Employees Have Substantial Control Over Work • Hierarchy Is Relatively Unimportant

Most technical leaders can't change things on the scale of say, General Motors. But you can change what you do and what those you work with every day do. It starts by moving away from an intimidating, rule-based approach where you feel your main task is to prevent people from making mistakes. You need to move to a style and approach that encourages people to grow and develop yet creates reasonable boundaries that ensure that their work stays consistent with the organizational goals that everyone will ultimately be judged against.

If, on the other hand, you work in a no-rule, no-process organization, you need to think carefully about creating and implementing more structure, particularly if the organization is growing and developing a larger reach. But, as you develop and implement rules, you must be wary of using rules as a substitute for leadership. There are always some people who will want to push for black-and-white, clear yes-and-no situations. These are rarely good for the business or for the people who make the business successful.

A Fourth Wave leader finds a way to maintain a dynamic and constructive balance between rules and culture.

THE PLAYBOOK

- Review your mission statement. Check with those you work with to see if it appeals to *their* ideals, hopes and dreams. If it doesn't, ask them to suggest how your mission statement can become more inspiring.
- Give employees the support and resources they need to do their jobs. When a problem arises, ask your team to list what they need. Certainly, there will be things on these lists that are impossible to obtain. You can't promise what you can't deliver, and you

shouldn't hesitate to say so. But that should help the list of needs become realistic and possible rather than an "I wish the world was perfect" fantasy.

- Empower employees to adjust to circumstances as they arise and not wait for orders from on high. Map major work processes and let everyone know that, as long as they follow the maps, they can do whatever is necessary. But also let them know that, if they think the map won't allow the results that are needed, they need to present this to the work team as a problem that requires assistance.

- Constant criticism can kill an organization. If you think that this is the norm in your work group, keep your own little tab during meetings. How many times do people criticize in these meetings? How many times do they praise someone or something? If the balance is poor, make sure you address this.

- Give more rewards and less disapproval. Support people when they are down and acknowledge their successes. Remember that punishment nearly always has unintended and unproductive consequences. Ask yourself a simple question, "Do I think this was a deliberate bit of sabotage, or was there something wrong with the process, resources, or assignment?" Deliberate sabotage arises so infrequently that you should assume it never occurs. Just suppose that everyone was trying to do the right thing as a starting point—this will help you keep your inner-alligator in check.

Behavior 3. Figure out where your role begins and ends.

In one of Rob's consulting engagements, he was asked to help because the CEO of a company—a talented entrepreneur—was so heavily micromanaging his staff that they were ready to revolt. He thought he could do anything better than anyone else. As a result, he wasn't letting anyone else do their job.

This was the classic situation of a young organic company that had slid into an autocratic structure.

Rob asked the CEO to complete a simple exercise in which he listed the duties his job description covered and those it didn't cover. Rob also asked his executive team to do the same thing because he wanted to see where there was agreement.

By the time the CEO finished, he'd listed 25 items–instead of the six or eight he should have had. Within six weeks, with Rob's coaching, he had found ways to feel comfortable letting go of details while clarifying his own vital role in the company. Rob showed him how to construct a daily schedule using pie charts to help him focus on four or five major tasks.

Letting go wasn't easy for him and he sometimes resisted strenuously, but he got the point, and things improved for everyone.

If you find that you are doing this, you need to get a better idea of what specifically needs to be done in your work. This could be a recurring set of tasks, which can be summed up in a set of process maps or flow charts. It could also be a one-time set of activities that must be completed, in the form of a project plan. In either case, the tasks must be associated with individuals. If you can build a coherent and written inventory of these issues, then you are much more likely to do what's necessary and not fall into the trap of micromanagement.

You can also deter and discourage those you work with from another thing that tech heads love to do—poaching the "fun" parts of any project or process from someone else.

THE PLAYBOOK

- As a supervisor or manager, sit down with each of your direct reports and ask them to work with you to make a list of "my job, not my job" activities. Note wherever a disconnect appears between your expectations and your subordinate's beliefs. (To do this properly, get the entire list from your report before you discuss any differences of opinion; if you don't, you'll choke off any kind of constructive discussion.) Then discuss how both of you can reach reasonable agreement on a revised list.

- Focus on what you can do, on tasks you can achieve, and situations you can influence. In addition, don't let things you can't do eat at your spirit.
    1. If you find that you've been given an assignment that you believe cannot be completed, break this down into parts that you can do and parts that you have doubts about.
    2. For each element or piece that you think can't be done, make a list of what it would take to overcome the roadblocks you think are likely.

3. Then, go through this with your teammates, and, after revision, review it with the person who gave you the assignment. Don't hesitate to ask for help. If you've done a good job in analyzing the situation, your boss won't think less of you; he or she will probably be impressed with your thorough and thoughtful approach.

Behavior 4. Control your temper.

One of the ugliest episodes in American business occurred when the Sunbeam-Oster Company self-destructed under the leadership of "Chainsaw Al" Dunlap. Dunlap, who had increased stock values at several companies with slash-and-burn techniques, was a dominating bully who often yelled, screamed, and even threw papers and other non-lethal objects at people. He wore a bullet-proof vest and carried a revolver wherever he went, and he felt it was necessary to have a personal bodyguard, too.

Eventually, Sunbeam collapsed under this pressure, as his subordinates engaged in dozens of questionable business practices and accounting tricks to cover up a simple fact: Dunlap's temper intimidated everyone, and they would do almost anything to avoid his anger.

Dunlap eventually agreed to pay a $15 million settlement in a shareholder lawsuit, and he further agreed to never again serve as an officer for a public company in the US.

Rarely does anyone relish a leader who can't control his temper. It's simply never appropriate or effective to get so exercised about something that you can't contain yourself. Angry explosions just scare people, and when they're scared, they're not productive. If you live in fear of the boss' wrath, you're working from a negative – "Let's not screw up or we're in for it" – instead of from a positive – "Let's do the best job we can and get the best results."

Few people can match Dunlap's volatility, but it's the little things that matter in most cases. When Mike was running his manufacturing company, he lost his temper when a new process—that Mike had personally devised and spent a relatively large amount of money to implement—didn't seem to work properly. The process required workers to load 50 parts into a simple fixture; if 49 or 51 were loaded, the parts would not meet customer requirements. However, this was a huge improvement over the previous process, where the workers had to complete a mathematical calculation, choose appropriate spacer plates, and assemble a multi-part fixture in an exact order to do the same job.

At first, things worked well. Everyone was happy—it was easy to run the new process, and all of the parts produced seemed to be acceptable. Soon, though, a batch of parts was found to be out of specification, and Mike was called to the shop to look into it.

"I'll bet there aren't 50 pieces in the fixture," Mike said. The worker replied that he had counted them carefully—but when the fixture was checked, there were only 48 pieces. Mike blew his top, asking sarcastically if the guy doing the job could count to 50.

That seemed to solve the problem, and Mike didn't hear about it again. Not, that is, until an irate customer called wanting to know why he had received a large number of parts that didn't meet requirements. Luckily for Mike, the supervisor of the work area was willing to challenge him and told Mike that nobody could count to 50 over and over again and get it right.

Mike took the challenge and agreed to work the job for a shift to prove it. In less than 2 hours, Mike had miscounted, too. Eventually, a sophisticated counting scale was used to make sure 50 parts were loaded in each fixture, and all seemed well.

Except for one thing: even though Mike realized he'd made a mistake, and publicly apologized for his loss of temper, everyone always talked about this episode. "Don't do that or Mike will yell at you," was almost legendary from that point forward.

People sometimes think it's good to get things off their chest and that doing so in anger will improve the situation. But in our view, anger makes matters worse almost every time. Some great coaches in American sports who were known for outbursts—Billy Martin, Bobby Knight and Woody Hayes, for example—might have been even more successful had they exhibited more control.

THE PLAYBOOK

- One of the best tools to manage anger is called RETHINK. Originally developed for parents, it works equally well in the workplace:
    1. RECOGNIZE what makes you angry. Are you hiding other emotions?
    2. EMPATHIZE with the other person—what is their view of the situation?
    3. THINK about the specific issue that made you angry.
    4. HEAR what the other person is saying. Look into their eyes and acknowledge that you hear them.

5. INTEGRATE respect into your response.

6. NOTICE your physical condition—heartbeat, breathing, tension in your neck, chest, and stomach.

7. KEEP your attention on the present—don't let past issues make you lose your temper.

- Maintain a "hostility log." This will teach you about the frequency and kinds of situations that provoke you and increase your awareness of what triggers these situations and how you can develop control. Use anger to warn you that it is time to reexamine your thinking about an issue, a comment, or a plan.

- Pinch your arms or do something that will distract you from the fight-or-flight response.

- Consider alternative explanations of an event that provokes you. You might be able to develop a better perspective and respond calmly.

- If you live each day as if it were your last, you will realize that life is too short to get angry over everything. Forgive those who have aroused you. If you can let go of resentment and stop looking for revenge, you'll find that the burden of anger can be lifted from you.

- You may need professional help if none of these other activities can stop your inner-alligator from jumping out.

Behavior 5. Feel the fear and do it anyway.

What distinguishes good leaders and entrepreneurs is that they feel fear, but they act anyway. Some like to think that great leaders are fearless. What we don't realize is that these folks have taught themselves to recognize that fear is not a red light but a caution light. You have a choice to proceed once you've assessed the situation and given yourself the signal to go ahead.

Andrew Grove, the genius who, with fellow PhD physicist Gordon Moore, built Intel into a world-class company, uses a famous saying that he turned into a book: "Only the Paranoid Survive." Intel, founded on memory chips, ran into trouble in 1984 when Asian manufacturers started clobbering Intel with lower prices and much shorter product development cycles.

At that point, Grove suggested Intel should concentrate exclusively on microprocessors, the heart of any computer, and drop the memory business entire. Moore, famous for Moore's Law, which says that the density of transistors on a chip will double every two years—meaning that memory power will grow exponentially with time—was dubious. After all, Intel was big, successful, and was still making a lot of money-making memory chips.

Grove's proposal was risky, but he asked Moore a simple question: if we were starting Intel today, would we make memory chips at all? Moore said no, and he and Grove were thereafter dedicated to making microprocessors. It's not a reach to say that Intel, as much as any firm, was been responsible for the computer revolution that followed. Their first commercial microprocessor, the 8086, was the basis for the IBM PC that drove personal computing from hobby status to iconic business tool and led to the proliferation of individual computing power we all use today—smartphones, tablets, laptops, and cloud computing.

Moore, the CEO when this occurred, had to feel the fear but proceed anyway.

Grove had to re-learn this again in 1994 when Intel released the then-new Pentium chip. Geeks found a flaw in the chip, in which certain complex calculations would be done incorrectly by the Pentium. Grove publicly stated that the possible error was so unlikely that only the most sophisticated high-end user would ever need to worry about it.

Soon, the technical community and the press were up in arms. Intel was condoning errors in the single piece of technology that most of the computer world was built on. After a brief but certainly terrible firestorm of bad publicity, Grove agreed to replace every single Pentium chip, even offering free home delivery for replacement chips. The total cost of this was $475 million, a huge number for Intel—or for almost any company in 1994.

However, the final picture turned out quite positive for Intel. Intel's reputation was not only saved, but Intel, which had never been well known outside of the geek community, was now famous. The "Intel Inside" advertising campaign followed, and Intel remains to this day a world leader in microprocessor development and sales.

Grove again had to be paranoid *and* he had to confront his fear. If the huge recall had failed, Intel could well have gone bankrupt and would probably have joined the long list of high-tech firms that have disappeared in some technical disaster. If he didn't act, the same result may well have ensued, but it would have been a slow and painful demise.

In our view, great leaders find things that are worth doing, and that usually means the tasks ahead will challenge you and kindle some fear. After all, if something is very safe, everyone would be doing it, and there wouldn't be much benefit in a goal that is "me too" and without risk.

THE PLAYBOOK

- Think hard about what you are afraid of and ask yourself: What's the worst that can happen if I do this? Then ask yourself: If the worst did happen, could I handle it? If that disturbs you, then prepare a contingency plan and be prepared to carry it out.

- Be aware that some of the best leaders in the world feel fear, just like you. Use fear as a positive motivator, not something that crushes your spirit. If you've started something that led to a bit of panic, take stock of the progress you are making on a regular basis. You may find that small bits of positive news will reframe your apprehension and calm your misgivings.

- Talk about your fears with others. You'll find that you're in good company. As Alan Mullaly, later CEO of Ford Motor Company, always told people when he was program manager for the Boeing 777 jetliner program—a program in which Boeing invested the total net worth of the company, in the middle of a major recession no less—it's OK to have a problem, it's OK to acknowledge that things are bad. Talk about the difficulties, understand what these events mean, and then go do what you need to do. When Boeing people did this, they were able to concentrate on their tasks, and, by almost any measure, the 777 program launch was (and remains today) the most successful in aerospace history.

Behavior 6. Think positive.

Many available studies suggest that companies that foster positive attitudes are the ones that weather the worst storms. Google seems to do a rather good job of it, for example, even though they've hit a few bumps in the road over time. But Google sailed through the economic crisis of 2008-2009 far better than most, and there's every reason to believe they'll come through the COVID-19 pandemic in good shape, too.

The Mackinac Bridge is an example of how engineers need to have a positive outlook. This suspension bridge, which joins Michigan's Lower and Upper Peninsulas across the treacherous Straits of Mackinac, is the ninth longest suspension bridge in the world and the longest in the Western Hemisphere.

It is extraordinary and without peer in many ways. First, it is the only major suspension bridge that isn't in a metropolitan area. Detroit is almost 275 miles away and Chicago is over 400 miles from the bridge. In addition, it's the only major suspension bridge anywhere that must face extremely harsh winter conditions, not to mention wind gusts that can reach 100 miles per hour.

The bridge was built in the 1950's and almost every expert said it couldn't be built. No one would provide financing, the ice floes in the Straits would crush any bridge, the ore freighters that traverse the Great Lakes would crash and destroy the pilings, the substrate beneath the bridge site was pockmarked with caves and would collapse under the weight of the bridge, and so forth. The wind was a particular challenge—everyone remembered the Tacoma Narrows Bridge, or "Galloping Gertie," that collapsed due to wind-induced vibrations not long after it was opened in 1940. Footage of that engineering failure is about as famous as any technical failure in history.

In fact, "Mighty Mac" was the first long suspension bridge built since "Galloping Gertie" collapsed. No investor wanted to sink money into another disaster like that one, and it took huge political will from the State of Michigan to get over that barrier.

One man, though, believed in the bridge—Dr. David B. Steinman, the designer of the bridge. Raised in the shadow of the Brooklyn Bridge in New York, Dr. Steinman had earned his doctoral degree from Columbia by the age of 20 and eventually went on to design more than 400 bridges. But none of his bridges were anything like the "Mighty Mac."

After designing many important bridges, including the Henry Hudson Bridge in New York, Steinman became interested in the Mackinac site. At the time, the only way to get from the southern half of Michigan to the northern half was either a ferry ride—which could take more than 24 hours due to queuing that would back up for 15 miles or more if the weather was bad, or an extremely long drive through Canada or Illinois and Wisconsin.

Steinman believed he could build a bridge, though, and without any support from any government or any investor, he surveyed the site and spent almost $250,000 of his own money, a princely sum at the time, to prepare preliminary designs and complete the important calculations. He started this work in 1943, just 3 years after the disaster in Tacoma.

Why did he do this? He wanted to build this bridge and felt this would be the crowning achievement of his career. Given Steinman's professional pride—he founded the National Society of Professional Engineers, the body behind engineering registration—it's also likely he wanted to restore public confidence in suspension bridges after the Tacoma Narrows collapse. He had a passion, he had a mission, and he had a spectacular vision of what he wanted to accomplish.

With Steinman's initial designs in hand, politicians in Michigan pulled together, and, with Steinman's drive and positive support, eventually found a way to issue and sell bonds to build the bridge. The bond issue was complex; interest started to accrue as soon as the bonds were issued, so every day that it took to build the bridge, the cost increased. And no construction would be possible during harsh northern Michigan winters, so there was tremendous pressure to meet or beat every deadline.

Steinman then led the project to completion, overcoming many complex and previously unmet challenges in constructing suspension bridges. Through it all, Steinman, a noticeably short man, was omnipresent and figuratively towered over one and all, urging them forward and stirring everyone involved to meet an extremely aggressive construction schedule.

When the bridge was opened in 1957, it was the longest suspension bridge in the world, a

standard that wasn't surpassed until 1998. The bonds were paid off well ahead of maturity, and none of the "doom and gloom" problems that all of the pundits said would make this bridge impossible have ever arisen on the bridge that Steinman developed and led to completion.

There were many great leaders who made the Mackinac Bridge possible, and five men were killed in accidents during construction. But without Steinman's positive, upbeat approach, this engineering sensation may never have built.

Even in lesser circumstances, positive and constructive attitudes can help anyone reach high level goals.

Keep in mind, though, that finding the bright side of the story doesn't mean you can ignore potential potholes and problems. For example, Steinman knew that the wind was a huge problem, and his design work, done with slide rules and adding machines—no computers were used—is estimated to be able to withstand winds of at least 150 miles per hour.

When Steinman was asked by a reporter what wind speed the bridge might withstand, Steinman is reputed to have said "An infinite wind."

That's optimism.

THE PLAYBOOK

- Talk to your team about ways to build a positive environment. Make every project a team project. If people have criticisms or concerns, take that as good news. You've found a potential problem, and you can develop a solution before things get out of hand.

- If someone constantly brings toxic emotions to the workplace, move that person out. One toxic person can poison the well. Studies have shown that as many as 85% of people that change jobs do so in part because they have to work with a negative person, and more than 93% of those surveyed reported that a "bad apple" has diminished their productivity.

- A leader's mood is contagious. Bring a positive mood to your job every day, but don't lose sight of reality. If you find that this is a challenge for you, once again, make a list of the things you want to promote every day. A key list of "talking points" is powerful in politics, and it can work for you, too.

Behavior 7. Get the help you need.

Most folks are willing to consult with an expert or get formal training when we're trying to learn a skill like golf, cooking, or a complicated home improvement technique. Sometimes we seek out other experts—therapists, coaches, and other external professionals—only when a situation appears to be an impossible mess. Too often, though, people—particularly technical people—don't seek help at all because they're fearful that this will be blot on their resume or because they feel shame that they are somehow flawed.

When Rob and Mike work with clients who are having problems with someone on their staff, the real issue is often driven by an individual who hasn't taken care of his or her personal problem. It may be that the person is depressed or anxious but not going to therapy. Or they may have anger problems and aren't getting coaching. Perhaps their finances are a mess but they haven't sought outside help. Untreated addictions are another huge concern.

If you've ever worked with someone who is in the middle of a difficult divorce, you've probably noticed that these people are rarely able to do their work properly. They usually have trouble working in teams due to the huge breach of trust that led to the divorce process.

Leaders need to support these people in dealing with the disruption. But it's always better to tackle your own problems. If you don't, things will almost always get worse.

The Second Law of Thermodynamics says that, unless you transfer substantial energy into a system, it will become more disorderly over time. The same principle applies to personal problems: unless you pour more energy than you have within your own psyche and knowledge base into the difficulty, it will get messier over time.

THE PLAYBOOK

- If you think you have a psychiatric problem, seek therapy.
- If you have a health problem, go to a doctor. Dental problems can also cause pain, misery, and even cardiovascular disease.
- If you're having trouble managing your work role, find and consult with a coach.
- If you've got an addiction, go to a 12-step meeting or talk to your physician.
- If there's trouble on the home front, go to a family therapist or marriage counselor.
- If you're having a spiritual crisis, seek out a member of the clergy.
- If you're not sure what you should do, consult a friend or someone close to you.
- Pray for guidance and remember the adage, "God helps those who help themselves."

Behavior 8. Play hard.

Keeping your balance also means you can't let your career control every waking moment of your life. Nor should you bury every one of your hopes and dreams in your family life—your partner and children need space to live their own lives, too.

Having fun is an essential element of good mental health, and Fourth Wave leaders know how to enjoy their lives. In fact, most of the successful entrepreneurs that Rob and Mike have encountered over the years will actually admit that their job is fun—they found something that they loved to do, and then turned that into an enterprise.

Few of us have had that experience, though, and even if you love your professional activities, you need to get away from it and do something that takes your mind away from your work environment. Stress and pressure aren't just things we feel in our minds. Stress also piles up chemical imbalances in your cardio-vascular system, and can be a major contributor to heart disease, strokes, and other serious or even fatal illnesses.

There's plenty of research to support the idea that having fun reduces these chemical imbalances, but almost everyone knows that if they take a break and do something that's just plain fun, they'll feel better. If you can get away from the stressful environment that most careers stew in today, you won't need a controlled study to know you have more energy, better concentration, and a renewed sense of purpose.

We do urge one note of caution, though. Don't just substitute "play stress" for "work stress." Too many people, particularly competitive people (and engineers can be extremely competitive), use the same take-no-prisoners, victory-at-all-cost attitude that they have in their career and apply this in recreational activities.

If you do this, you'll get far less benefit. It may also annoy your family, and, if you happen to have friends in both the work and play spheres of your life, you'll find that most of them won't appreciate your off-duty attitude back in the office, factory, or on a job site.

THE PLAYBOOK

- Find a hobby or other endeavor that separates you from your daily routine and replenishes your energy and spirit. You'll get a double benefit if this involves physical activity, but a sense of rejuvenation is more important than sore muscles.

- Make a conscious effort to put non-work activities on your calendar. Software tools are available to synchronize two calendars, so if you are limited by security rules from adding these to your work calendar, look for one of these tools.

- Don't work while on vacation; don't think about work when you're at play. You may have a need to check your email, but you may not. Mike worked with one executive who, upon departing for vacation, set up his "out of office" message and then didn't open up a single email while out having a good time. Upon his return, he would, without looking at a single email, delete everything in his in-box. He explained it this way, "If it's really important, they'll send another note. If it was an emergency, it's already over."

- Join an adult sports league or activity group. Having fun in a group can lift your spirits. If this is tied to your job, make sure you keep a sense of proportion about the games. Winning with your work mates can be a great team building experience but losing—not to mention behaving badly when losing—can be quite negative.

- Make a plan for the weekend ahead so everyone in the family is excited about it. But *put it on your calendar so you manage your time, just as you would any important meeting!*

Behavior 9. Manage your energy as well as your time.

Time is the most democratic thing on earth. Every single person gets 24 hours each day. Some are blessed with more days than others, but each day is the same for every man, woman, and child on the planet.

When people say they don't have enough time, it might be more accurate to say that they don't have enough energy. In some ways, time and energy can be exchanged. You can't get more time from greater energy, but you can get more done in the time you have if you have more get-up-and-go. If you're too tired to perform in your job or to interact with your family, more time alone probably won't address that imbalance.

However, you can't manufacture time, and, at some point, you will need to see what you can do to generate more energy to use your time more effectively. To start, you should ask yourself if you're getting enough sleep, enough recreation away from work, enough family time, and enough exercise.

Too often, most of us find that sleep and exercise are the first things that drop off our list of things to do when time is tight. While it may not be possible to get enough sleep every day, if you find that you are cheating yourself on sleep regularly, you simply must re-order some of your priorities.

Adding a short period of exercise to your day will almost always increase your energy level. This doesn't have to turn into training for 10K runs or marathons; just a short 20 minute walk will likely bring you renewed vigor and concentration, not to mention big health benefits if done regularly.

If you are having difficulties in your personal life, consider getting professional assistance. Or, you simply may need to do without some television program to spend time with your children. While television can be a great teaching tool, even the most educational shows allow you to sit passively. (Mike can't count the number of times he's fallen asleep watching PBS's *Nova*, even though it's one of the most engrossing science shows on the tube.)

It's extremely important to avoid the burnout that so often ensnares people in challenging roles.

As a leader, it's a fool's bet to continually prove your worth with a superhuman effort or by trying to amaze others with your time commitment.

Formula 1 drivers accelerate and decelerate faster than any other motor sports contestants. However, to win in this über-competitive arena, you have to manage your fuel. If you use it too fast, you may lead for a while. Then, though, you'll have to pit sooner and possibly more often than everyone else and you'll find yourself behind at the end of the race. Or, you might run out of gas and not even finish the race.

You need to be fast but you also need to have a sustainable style—just as you must to be a Fourth Wave leader.

Managing time often is really about managing energy. It's not just becoming more efficient. People often will try to do two things at once – take calls in the car while driving home, for example. But others may use the drive home to unwind and recharge. They don't have to plop down in a chair and find they don't have enough energy to fulfill home-based responsibilities.

You really can't cheat time. We all have our limits.

THE PLAYBOOK

- Layout and prepare your clothes for the morning *before* you go to bed. You'd be surprised at how much easier this is than scrambling around, unable to find what you are looking for when you know you have a deadline to start your day.

- Get a coffee maker with a timer and learn how to use it. Set it up in the evening and enjoy hot coffee in the morning. Stopping for a custom-prepared latte every morning is not only expensive, but it's often a drag on your time. What could you do with an extra 15 minutes every morning? You can probably treat yourself to a tall half-skinny half 1 percent extra hot split quad shot (two shots decaf, two shots regular) latte with whip once in a while, but if you do this every day, it will eat into your 24-hour allotment.

- Keep an energy journal so you can zero in on when you lose your energy and when it's at a peak. Journal the events or activities that boost you into high-energy moments. Accept that you need these stimuli to boost your energy.

- Meditate. If you don't know how, many school districts offer low-cost adult education programs where you can learn some form of meditative activity. There are numerous apps that can do the same thing.

- Get regular exercise, even if it's brief. If you hate exercise, see if you can find someone who'll join you every day for a short walk—even if that "someone" is just your dog. Perhaps you just need to use the stairs to get to your fifth floor office every day. If you have trouble doing this, put the time on your calendar and make it part of your schedule.

- If your commute wears you out on a regular basis, you may be suffering from low-grade carbon monoxide poisoning. Breathing exhaust fumes in bumper-to-bumper traffic day in and day out is more debilitating than most people realize. Consider taking alternative routes where you keep moving even if the trip takes 10 more minutes.

Behavior 10. Avoid cutoffs. Don't ghost anyone.

We talked about the flight-or-fight syndrome back in Chapter 1. And, through most of the Clipboard-Playbook entries, we've tried to provide you with suggestions on how you can avoid the fight response when stress hits.

Even if you manage to control your inner-alligator, your inner-turtle might pop out. Sometimes, this is just as simple as walking away when you are angry, but it can grow into a consistent effort to avoid someone. In the worst case, this can become a full-fledged emotional cutoff.

Cutting someone off cold, or ghosting them, is a hard-wired coping mechanism that is part of survival for higher forms of life, and we find that people invoke this response in their career as well as in their personal affairs.

When you do this, you are, in effect, punishing the other party. They won't have any way to try to fix the relationship because you deny them access. On the other hand, someone who initiates a cutoff creates a self-inflicted wound of sorts because they invariably isolate themselves more and more as time goes on. They never really work through a conflict; they use cutoffs as their means to "resolve" the situation.

Of course, cutoffs arise from something that was unpleasant, probably for both sides. Holding on to a grudge is a likely way to build stress and insure that whatever went wrong will continue to exact a price in your health, energy, and the joy of living. As William Faulkner wrote, "The past is not dead. In fact, it's not even past."

In organizations, cutoffs are usually associated with serious feuds. As a leader, you can't allow yourself to do this. Difficult as it may be, you need to find a way to constructively engage someone who has made you angry and try to do this in a way that is constructive.

Rick Brenner, a physicist, electrical engineer, and software engineer from Boston who consults with technical organizations, notes that a feud "acts like the Blob of sci-fi films...anything the organization tries to accomplish is potential nourishment for the dispute. In a workplace dominated by feuds, people cannot take pride in their work. Their health suffers, and the best workers—those who have alternatives—leave."

Cutoffs are rarely helpful—they give some temporary relief from an unhappy conflict, but the resentment and distaste always remain. There might be an exception when there is a threat of violence, but even the most bitter of rivals may find a way to interact with the other person in a safer public setting.

THE PLAYBOOK

- If you need a cooling-off period from a difficult relationship, take a time out but let the person know that you'll be in touch at some point in the future. Then set a review date and assess the situation again at that time. Don't just say "sometime in the future" and use that as an excuse or an easy way to continue the cutoff. You don't need to commit to the future date with the other party, but you need to make a personal commitment to revisit the situation within a definite timeframe.

- If two people who work for you are engaged in a cutoff, formally plan and then hold a sit-down session in which you specifically list both sides' complaints, and then help find some sort of middle ground. As a leader, you should be able to do this for all but the most severe feuds. And, at some point, if you find that one of the parties is simply unable to get over their anger, you may need to move them out of the organization.

- Keep in contact through written communication if nothing else. However, don't indulge in false apologies to keep this going. Here are some sentiments that are used far too often once emotional damage has set in—we call these "non-apology apologies:"

    1. I'm sorry you feel that way.
    2. I'm sorry you got mad.
    3. I'm sorry, but I don't really care what you think at this point.
    4. I'm sorry that you think this is so important.
    5. I'm sorry you misunderstood.

- Seek therapy from a professional or advice from your spiritual advisor if you feel it is warranted. Don't continue the isolation—you are punishing yourself as much as anyone.

Behavior 11. Take good care of yourself.

When your health is less than it could be, your ability to be an effective leader will be impaired. If you have the misfortune to spend more than three days as a hospital patient, you will know it deep in your bones. When you return to work, you're almost sure to find your stamina, energy, and concentration are negatively affected, and it takes time to recover.

Some research suggests that good economic times promote bad habits—people tend to drink too much, eat too much and slack off on exercise. Though the evidence is mixed about the opposite situation—whether bad times can be good for you—by maintaining good habits in good times, you'll find your habits are more likely to stick with you when times are tough.

Your body is a complex system, and, like any complex device, it requires good maintenance and the right fuel to function properly. If you have a car and you don't change the oil regularly, you will pay a price later, either in scrapping the car well short of its normal life, or with expensive repairs. You need to use the right grade of fuel, and be wary of nicks and scratches turning into rust.

It's no different with your health. Cheat now and you'll surely pay later. Change your oil and your filters; rotate your tires and wash the road grime away from your life. We hardly need to say this, but we certainly hope you're not scrapped prematurely; it's impossible to lead from the grave.

As Mike will freely attest, there's nothing that will remind you of the importance of good personal habits better than lying on an operating table, watching a cardiac surgeon do a roto-rooter job—an angioplasty—on your heart. (The entire procedure is visible on large electronic displays in many operating theaters—the surgeon literally performs the procedure by watching the screen, and the patient can see the screens, too.)

If you know what's going on, you realize you could be dead shortly after the surgeon said "oops" but before you knew what happened. This tends to be a strong motivation to improve your personal eating and exercise habits, and makes you willing to visit a physician from time to time.

THE PLAYBOOK

- Develop routines that promote good health: regular exercise, a sound diet, and regular visits to your health care providers. If you are having difficulty keeping to a regular schedule, once again we recommend using your personal calendar system to overcome the imbalance that you've developed.
- Control your use of alcohol. Find another activity one or two nights a week instead of an evening drink. Be particularly wary of drinking at lunch. There can be a great deal of pressure to do so in certain business situations.
- Give up a bad habit. Make a plan, commit to it and be willing to be accountable to someone else. If you use tobacco, just remember that the negatives so greatly outweigh the positives that you need to quit. It isn't a sign of weaknesses to get medical help. There are reams of research that show that nicotine is at least as addictive as cocaine. Once you've gotten hooked, only a small percentage of people who try to quit without assistance are successful.
- Get a good quality scale and monitor your weight on a regular basis. If you start to gain weight in the winter—as many people do—keep a log of what you

eat. There are a number of free tools or apps that are readily available to help you with this. You'll be surprised at how many calories you are consuming if you keep an honest tab of what you thrust into your mouth!

- If you travel a great deal and have to eat in restaurants frequently, try to eat half of what you order and take the rest home in a box or doggie bag. Many entrees have twice as many calories as you need in a single meal. Again, a good habit can save you money while giving you a time saving meal— nothing but microwave skills are needed to heat up a satisfying box of leftovers.

- Be careful when ordering lunch at business meetings, or when lunch is brought in for an in-house gathering. The temptation to overeat when someone else is paying is great, as is the likelihood that the food you'll see has several less-than-healthy attributes. This is another transition point, and if you don't think about this until the greasy pizza shows up, you may find yourself gorging on something you probably shouldn't. The omnipresent giant cookies are also great but not the best thing if you're trying to control your weight and/or your cholesterol and body fat.

- Don't skip breakfast; almost all structured nutrition programs include a good morning meal for a reason. Failure to eat after a full night of sleep, even if your appetite can be temporarily suppressed with caffeine, causes almost everyone to eat too much later in the day. If you have trouble preparing something reasonable when you rise and can't seem to shine, set up your meal in the evening and you'll find this takes most of the inconvenience out of doing something good for yourself.

Behavior 12. Be disciplined.

Almost everyone who achieves a reasonable degree of tasks and relationship balance has to wield discipline in their life. It's rare to find anyone who does this effortlessly, so if you find that you struggle, don't worry. Struggling to maintain control is perfectly natural.

However, you don't have to do this by simple will power alone in the 21st century. There are plenty of inexpensive apps that can help you set up, maintain, and continually improve self-discipline in your work as well as your personal life.

The poet Maya Angelou framed this issue well when she said, "Some people regard discipline as a chore. For me, it is a kind of order that sets me free to fly."

This is really fundamental. If you can do the things you always <u>need</u> to do without needless concentration and effort, you have much more time and energy to do the things you <u>want</u> to do. We think it's hard to conceive of a balanced leader who can't maintain personal control—or self-discipline.

THE PLAYBOOK

- Electronic calendars or detailed pen-and-paper planners are some of the most powerful tools that a modern leader needs to master. If you use one, spend time every day maintaining it. If you don't, pick one you like and learn to use it.
- Delegate effectively as a leader. Giving your reports meaningful work is a powerful way to develop their skills—and to build discipline and structure into everyone's work. If you try to do it all yourself, you'll

soon become that business horror, a micromanager. Just remember that delegation is the personal loan of authority—but you really can't loan out your responsibility. Once you delegate, make sure you follow up regularly (but don't snoop) and offer to help anyone who's having trouble getting something done. Don't fool yourself into thinking that nobody can make a contribution at work that's as good as yours. People who think this way inevitably end up being ineffective because they're tired, grumpy and burned out.

- Remember that almost any new routine needs time to be successful. It's unlikely you learned to ride a bicycle the first time you hopped on a two wheeler, but once things clicked, you had a skill that's lasted all your life.

- Periodically clean your desk or work area. It doesn't have to be a sterile, featureless expanse, but the Japanese "Five S" routine is worth considering for your own personal workspace a simple reason: if you can master the discipline of the Five S system, you will be more productive in your job—and this works at home, too. The Five S system is based on these ideas:

    1. *Sort (Seiri)*
        - Disorderly work areas hide problems in your work; Keep only what is needed for your tasks
    2. *Set In Order (Seiton)*
        - Make it easy to find what is needed—and to see what might go wrong
    3. *Shine (Seiso)*

- Trash, dust, and grime disguise inefficiencies and lead to confusion

4. *Standardize (Seiketsu)*
    - Schedules and methods of performing cleaning, sorting, & organization keep order on a regular basis

5. *Sustain (Shitsuke)*
    - Regular organization of your work area helps you improve your work habits on a repeated basis, which is the essence of continual improvement

Behavior 13. Build free days into your schedule.

Young adults who've entered the work force in the past two decades have enjoyed the highest standard of living of any generational cohort in history. They've also lived the most structured childhood of any generation—their play was largely organized, with play dates, soccer leagues, and other activities that grown-ups planned and tightly supervised.

With this background, free and unfettered days can seem alien, like visiting a foreign country. And yet almost no one can stay in high gear forever without suffering the consequences. In the go-go days of the dot-com boom, where Generation Xer's honed their work habits—which seems like ancient history to the now maturing Millennials—people everywhere were talking about the new 24-7 work world. Newspapers (how quaint) and magazines (ditto) were full of stories about startup companies where people worked for 2 or 3 days without stopping, fueled by coffee and wild dreams, to create breakthrough business opportunities.

Of course, this pace couldn't be sustained. Not only did the dot-com boom go bust, the Gen X players who engaged and fed those hectic and exciting times, simply could not continue that pace. This approach to a career is unsustainable, and highly imbalanced.

However, there's nothing particularly magical about the year you were born in when it comes to non-stop work. No one can go on indefinitely, and those who try often suffer spectacular cases of burn-out that can take years to recover from. A rapidly spinning wheel that's out of balance will soon start to vibrate uncontrollably. The bearings that support the wheel are quickly damaged, and, if the bearings seize, the wheel can explode with great force.

Career burn-out can be a lot like that.

To prevent this—and to stay balanced—you need to make sure you take time to plug in and recharge. You need to spin your wheel down once in a while, trim the excesses away, and, if you do, you just might find that you can spin it at an even higher speed once the refurbishment is complete.

THE PLAYBOOK

- When you conduct quarterly calendar reviews, count how many free days you've enjoyed in the past three months. Now, sit down and figure out how many you want to take in the year ahead. Put them into your schedule, and guard them carefully. If you simply must work on one of these days, reschedule the free day just as you would any other important event that gets changed.

- Plan a special trip with your partner and/or family–one you can't easily cancel–and make the reservations so you're locked in.

- On one of your free days, sign up for community service activities that have nothing to do with your work. If this can further your vision and address your personal mission—without reminding you of your career—so much the better.

- On free days, set up lunch or dinner dates with old friends to reconnect and catch up. If you have trouble doing this, get out an old yearbook or look at one of the "alumni" social sites online. Review the list of names and see if a memory stirs you to re-establish contact.

- Don't hesitate to simply sit and relax once in a while. Painting the bedroom or working on your latest assignment can wait. If you had a heart attack, you might end up in intensive care for several days and the world would continue to spin.

Behavior 14. Reject the tyranny of a totally-wired world.

Jean-Jacques Rousseau said, "Man is born free, and everywhere he is in chains." No kidding! Today's chains are digital and wireless…

There's a reason that some early smart phones were once known as "Crackberries." Smart phones really are addictive. Many who use phones or tablets intensively find a huge level of exhilaration, excitement, and sheer pleasure from the feeling of being connected and needed at all times.

The perception that you are somehow indispensable is yet another self-defeating illusion. Like most addictions, the initial rush soon requires higher and higher doses to get the same effect. Without noticing, addicts soon find that they are on a treadmill and they are chasing an unattainable goal. Again, the result is a crash, often of mammoth proportion.

One of Verizon's television commercials from several years ago, when phones were becoming true handheld computers, showed a man at a picnic, surrounded by friends and family. He talks about his friend, who's like a brother to him, and his brother, who's more like a cousin. At the end of the commercial, he asks the Verizon network horde, led by the now-semi famous "can you hear me now" guy, if he can enjoy unlimited talk time with all of them.

Of course, the answer is yes. If you watch this commercial several times, you start to notice how annoying everyone at the picnic seems to be, and a simple retort might pop into your head. Yes, you <u>could</u> talk to them without limit, but *why would you want to*?

It's not a reach to understand why a fifteen-year-old might desire unlimited texting, non-stop talking, and, if they could get it, a hardwired neuro-link to all of their friends. This is a great way to wall off the adult world, and to do what adolescents have always done, namely explore their options and develop an identity that's separate from their parents.

However, why would a 27-year old—or 48-year-old—adult want to do that? For many people, the reasons are similar, but more complex, too. When this type of connection with your professional persona becomes non-stop, it's not possible to believe that the victim of this self-induced compulsion has a reasonable degree of balance in their life.

No matter—once the rush of adrenaline starts, the reaction is really no different than the bliss a heroin addict feels when the needle slips into a vein. And, like junkies, electronic addicts love to gather and convince themselves that their behavior is somehow normal and balanced.

There are good and constructive uses for smart phones, tablets, and the like (even to talk to your family at length). But if the need to be connected becomes compulsive, you have fallen badly out of balance and need to inject a conscious and determined effort into bringing your life back into equilibrium.

THE PLAYBOOK

- Use a screen time app to monitor your usage. There really is an "off" switch—trust us on this one.
- You don't have to check your e-mail every minute. Email notification features aren't much different from the bell that Pavlov used to make dogs salivate.
- Take a vacation where cell reception is weak or non-existent.
- Let people know that you will not be checking your e-mail or phone after a certain time each day.
- Put your phone away when meeting with people or turn it off completely. Don't just put it on vibrate. If you simply must have it on, find the "silent" setting and don't fret that you'll miss something.

CHAPTER SEVEN

The Coach's Clipboard: Your Enthusiasm Springs from Within...

Influential people don't get to that station in life by sitting. They're active. They get involved in wide-ranging areas that interest them. Fueled by a powerful mission in life, they seem to have more energy than most of the people around them.

If you watch any US Presidential election, no matter who you may favor, it is utterly amazing to observe the incredibly high levels of energy and enthusiasm that candidates exhibit almost every day. In fact, some of the candidates who don't reach the final round either drop out or are forced out because the voting public can see that their gusto was gone at some key point. It may be fleeting and not permanent, but American voters are sensitive to this kind of reaction.

How can someone maintain an almost limitless level of fervor over a grueling two year period of virtually non-stop personal appearances, 18 hour days, and more 7 day work periods than most of us could endure? Most of us can't—we sometimes get stuck—and we need to rekindle the fire, even if we don't have a mission as large as running a major government.

Let's take a look at some of the factors that can keep you going. You don't need to demonstrate that you are capable of holding the office of President of the United States, but you do need to continually demonstrate that you are engaged, interested, and enthusiastic—even when, deep inside, you may not feel excited or moved by what you are doing at the moment.

How can you keep your internal fire smoldering, or even fully ablaze, most of the time?

Behavior 1. Have a dream.

The future belongs to those who believe in the beauty of their dreams.
—Eleanor Roosevelt

Goals are important, but successful leaders are rarely content with simple, finite goals. The leaders who leave footprints for future generations are motivated by dreams. Jim Collins and Jerry Porras, in "Built To Last," their study of long-term business success, coined a term for outsized dreams. They called a grand dream a BHAG: a big, hairy, audacious goal.

In 2008, the National Academy of Engineering completed a detailed study about the future. This study identified fourteen technically driven "Grand Challenges" for the 21st century.

They followed that with an ongoing initiative to stimulate, support, and inspire the up and coming generations of engineers, technologists, and scientists. The original list is unchanged in 2020—and, as you will see, these goals have remained enduring, stimulating and worthy of continued efforts in the advancement of technology.

Note that there has been some real progress on most of these goals during the past twelve years, but not one has been fully realized. That's evidence they really are BHAG's:[3]

1. Advance Personalized Learning
2. Make solar energy economical
3. Enhance virtual reality
4. Reverse-engineer the brain
5. Engineer better medicines
6. Advance health informatics
7. Restore and improve urban infrastructure
8. Secure cyberspace
9. Create wide access to clean water
10. Generate energy from fusion
11. Prevent nuclear terror
12. Manage the nitrogen cycle
13. Develop carbon sequestration methods
14. Engineer the tools of scientific discovery

If one of these topics doesn't inspire you, perhaps something else will. It might even be that something on this list makes you angry or irritated, which may lead to a dream. What can you contribute—other than simple criticism—that will do something positive for others?

---

[3] The National Academy of Engineering,
http://www.engineeringchallenges.org/challenges.aspx

THE PLAYBOOK

- Anyone who is serious about being a leader has dreams. You may have to set your ideas down in writing before you realize they are in your mind. If you're unclear about why you put one foot in front of the other every day, revisit your mission and vision statements. See if they still make sense, but more importantly, see if they inspire you. If they don't, consider changing these statements. Then, do something to turn these dreams into reality.

- There are many places in your life where a dream can develop:

    1. Formulate a dream about your company with colleagues, and then develop a plan to achieve an initial step in this vision.

    2. Devise a dream about something wonderful to strive for with your family. Perhaps you have a special trip in mind, or you envisage your children attending a top-notch university.

    3. Dream about where your life is headed with your significant other. Too many relationships founder on the rocks of boredom; is your relationship docked in a harbor, waiting to be buffeted and perhaps destroyed when a big storm blows in?

    4. Have a vision about what you want to look like. First, look in the mirror. Then, think about how you might feel if you looked differently. This doesn't mean you need plastic surgery. Losing a few pounds or changing your hairstyle might make a huge difference in the way others see you, and

make you feel better about yourself at the same time.

- Visualize the future if you could change the way the world works. Don't allow the past to be a prison cell and don't think you have to change everything to make a splash; think about one aspect of life that you think can and should be better. What could you do to make that happen? Tell others about your dream and try and interest them in helping you act on these dreams. Very few people can make a BHAG into reality without help.

Behavior 2. Commit to your dream.

Don't be afraid to take a big step if one is indicated. You can't cross a great chasm in two small jumps.
David Lloyd George, British Prime Minister 1916-1922

One of the most profound principles that Mike and Rob have discovered in their work with organizations can be found in something called the "change equation."

This equation, which was originally proposed by Richard Beckhard and David Gleicher, says that the potential for any change to become reality is affected four factors:

- The level of dissatisfaction that exists with the status quo (D)
- The vision of what the future will be like—after the change becomes reality (V)
- The likelihood that meaningful first steps of the change can be accomplished (F)
- The level of resistance that exists among those affected by the possible change (R)

The change equation then suggests that just a small amount of resistance can overwhelm the other factors:

$$D * V * F > R$$

Of course, it's not realistic to expect that you can put numbers on each of these factors and thereby calculate some specific probability that a dream will become reality. However, this is an extremely powerful concept because it does show an apparently inescapable principle.

If any of the first three factors—dissatisfaction with the way things are today, vision, or first step probability—is close to zero or negative, the impetus for change will be close to zero or negative. As a result, even the smallest level of resistance will render the change impossible. Just one—not all—of the factors at or near zero will insure that resistance will win.

In Star Trek's *The Next Generation* series, Captain Picard and his crew are frequently engaged in life and death—or perhaps worse than death, technological enslavement—struggles with a consortium of beings known as "The Borg." Short for cybernetic organism, or cyborg, this polyglot empire seeks to "assimilate" all intelligent life (and their associated technology) into their collectivist domain.

The Borg's signature salutation is simple. "You will be assimilated. *Resistance is futile.*" Of course, the earthlings and their allies resist—and the resistance is <u>always</u> successful in the end.

If you follow the plots of these episodes, you quickly understand that the earthlings are not dissatisfied with the status quo (particularly so if the Borg would stop trying to devour their souls), and they have distinctly negative feelings about the Borg vision of the future. No matter that the achievable first steps—turning each earthling into an electro-mechanical zombie—is all too easy; the fact that "D" is effectively zero makes resistance powerful and effective.

This means you need to have a positive, constructive dream. You can't just be against something; your dream needs to be about upbeat and beneficial change. It also means that you must be prepared to face resistance. Finally, it also means that you have to jump in with both feet if you really expect to achieve something significant.

If you think about the COVID-19 pandemic, you'll see the change equation at work. There was little dissatisfaction with the status quo when the outbreak began. In nearly every country (save Taiwan and Singapore, where the memories of the 2003 SARS epidemics were still painful), it took significant tragedy and suffering—massive dissatisfaction—to overcome resistance to change. Even then, without achievable action plans, or a vision of how things could be better in the future, many places and people in the world still resisted change.

The dream you have, no matter how inspirational your idea, just isn't enough if people are happy with the way things are.

The key conclusion that you need to draw is crystal clear. Resistance is *natural and expected* whenever you are leading the clarion call to change something. Crushing or pushing back against resistance doesn't work because resistance is <u>not</u> futile; it works amazingly well.

To overcome these hurdles, you must be prepared to work hard, and to face peril. Moreover, if your dream is truly a Big Hairy Audacious Goal, or BHAG, then you will realize you can't wade in raging surf.

On the north shore of the island of Oahu in Hawaii in January, huge waves are the norm. It's dangerous to just get a bit wet because there's also an extremely strong riptide that can easily sweep you out to sea if you simply walk on wet sand. If you get close to the water, the next wave can unexpectedly arc over you without much warning. You need to be ready to swim as if your life depended on it, because it does.

If you aren't ready to swim for your life, you can't get just a little bit wet.

THE PLAYBOOK

- Recognize the distinction between a to-do list and a dream. A dream is bigger. You have to feel some passion for it. It's the kind of thing that makes you nervous. You know it's not going to be easy. But no dream is going to come true by accident. You're going to have to dig deep for it and risk something.

- Don't just go through the motions. If you aren't risking something, there's unlikely to be any significant reward. If this bothers you, review the Clipboard discussion and Playbook suggestions in Chapter 6 for "Feel the fear and do it anyway."

- Develop a plan and implement it. You don't need a perfect plan to succeed, just a good one executed with reasonable precision. Ask critical questions and try and develop this plan with friends, allies, and those who share the dream:

    1. What are the dissatisfactions that this dream deals with? If everyone loves what they have today, why would they want what your dream promises?

2. What vision are we offering of a better future? Can we explain this vision? Is it practical? Don't expect unanimous support, and plan to promote and sell your ideas. Trust us; few visions are so wonderful that they sell themselves. You have to work very hard just to get people to notice what you have proposed.

3. Does your plan include some initial actions that are likely to succeed? If you can't show other people that you can execute something simple, they won't believe you can achieve a BHAG.

4. When making decisions, ask yourself: Am I running away from something or toward something? Toward is always better, because resistance isn't pointless. That means working on the positive side of the ledger rather than browbeating people about negatives. You can list the reasons why people will resist your ideas, but don't fool yourself into thinking that you can dissuade them from believing in these negatives. Instead, fill the agenda of your plan with things that will accentuate the positive—run toward something that's appealing, not away from something negative.

5. Often, you need to educate others to make them feel dissatisfaction with the current state of affairs. This is tricky—if you become a naysayer or prophet of doom, you'll still end up with nothing but a dream gone sour. If you can put facts on the table, over time you may well be able to make people realize they have been lulled by complacency, and

storms are brewing over the horizon. They may not know it, and you need to create awareness of the risks that are likely and lay out why they *should* be dissatisfied with the status quo. And this is hard, because any prediction about the future is certain to be less than 100% accurate. But you need to do this with a minimum of negativity.

Behavior 3. Define your passion.

Some people think that Bill Gates has led an enchanted life. Well, if you look into the details of his time on earth, it's likely that most of you would say, yes, he *has* enjoyed a truly fortunate existence.

Gates was born into a well-to-do family. His father was a lawyer, his maternal grandfather was a bank president, and he attended some of the best schools in the Seattle area as a boy. At 13, Gates was enrolled at Lakeside School, a private prep school with an endowment larger than many small colleges.

However, Gates wasn't just along for the ride. When the Lakeside Mother's Club bought a dumb terminal and some network time to use it—not a common thing at the time—Gates quickly became captivated by the technology. With Paul Allen, he wrote a simple tic-tac-toe program, a real achievement at a time when computer or video games simply didn't exist.

Soon, Gates had gone beyond the simple things he could do with a teletype terminal, and, with Allen and other Lakeside students, he wheedled a local company into allowing them to play with a DEC PDP-11 minicomputer, the first non-mainframe computer that was commercially successful. It wasn't long before the company booted them out for what is today called "hacking"—the gang had found a way to get additional free time on the machine by exploiting security bugs and were caught.

But Gates didn't slink away. He had the nerve to offer his services to the company, to find the flaws in their programs and help them improve their system. They agreed, and he continued doing this until, when he was 15, the company went out of business. (There's no evidence, and no one has even suggested that Gates had anything to do with the failure.)

After gaining a near-perfect score on the SAT exam, Gates headed east to Harvard, but spent most of his time playing with the campus computers. Two years into his college career, Gates persuaded his parents to let him drop out to start a software company in partnership with Allen.

It wasn't long before Micro-Soft became Microsoft—and Gates, like Andy Grove and Gordon Moore at Intel—bet everything on the IBM PC of the mid 80's. The MS-DOS operating system was the result, and most people know the ensuing history.

The point is simple: Gates knew what his passion was, and he pursued it both with dedication and an air of confidence that was really above and beyond the norm. When you step back and look at this, you find there are a few key points that were critical in Gates' professional successes.

Fundamentally, he knew what he wanted to do, and he was clearly driven by it, almost (but not quite) obsessed by his dream. He also realized he had a special talent in programming, and he disregarded what could have been a quiet life of privilege to pursue it. Dropping out of Harvard to write obscure computer programs (when computers weren't very important in the scheme of things) with your teenage buddy? How many of us would be happy if our son or daughter told us they were going to do something like that?

Many years later, when Microsoft became a behemoth that enraged geeks around the world, Gates eventually realized that he had reached a level of achievement that was satisfying to him. Since then, he has continued to participate in Microsoft's affairs, because he remains passionate about the role of technology in peoples' lives, but he has also spent a great deal of time and money as a philanthropist through the Bill and Melinda Gates Foundation.

Charmed? It's hard to say no. But predestined and without setbacks along the way? Without the focus and drive that Gates had, it's not easy to imagine how anyone could have had the success he's enjoyed. We also think that Gates may well leave behind some of the largest and most impressive footprints of any human in history when all is said and done.

More significantly, anyone who reads the "15 Guiding Principles" of the Gates Foundation would be equally hard pressed to deny that this is a charter for achieving great things. If you don't know much about this, Google on "Bill and Melinda Gates Foundation" (what would someone have thought that phrase meant in 1975 when Gates dropped out of Harvard?) and see what you can learn.

THE PLAYBOOK

- Being "best in the world" is a tall order, but if you think about "your world" as opposed to "the whole wide world," it becomes more comprehensible and easier to dream about. What about "best in your company" or "best in your class." Try and state your enthusiasm in terms of your reach, but don't hesitate to go after something right at the end of your outstretched hands.

- Identifying what you *aren't* best at, and probably never will be, is just as important. Too often we spend too much time striving to overcome our weaknesses instead of developing our strengths. If you're five foot six, can't jump very high, and have small hands, you're unlikely to be a superstar on the basketball court. However, you might be the next legendary bridge engineer, like David Steinman.

- Develop yourself and your team. Each day, ask yourself: Have I mentored someone or contributed in some way to the development of others? One of the greatest footprints you can leave is the betterment of people around you. In the final earthly ledger, that's the thing that will be most important to those who remember your life.

- If your passion belongs to you and you alone, you aren't likely to see it take flight. You need to excite others. In today's connected, wireless world, there are so many ways to find friends and allies. Join a group, participate in a social networking site, write a blog, or launch your own web site. If you really believe, none of this will be impossible.

Behavior 4. Accept your leadership role.

Being a leader also requires that you step up to challenges that come your way. It's OK to be modest and self-effacing—it's even OK to laugh at yourself from time to time. However, at some point, you can't expand your influence unless you stand up and act the part. However, like most things related to tasks and relationship balances, this isn't as easy as it might seem.

Part of leadership is looking the part. How do you dress? Is your personal hygiene reflective of the role you see yourself playing? Is your physical posture consistent with the expectations that others have of a leader? In "As You Like It," Shakespeare described this well:

> ***All the world's a stage,***
> ***And all the men and women merely players;***
> ***They have their exits and their entrances,***
> ***And one man in his time plays many parts***

Playing your part is an essential aspect of leadership. One executive that Mike worked with—we'll call him Roy—had learned this lesson well and could quickly adapt to many circumstances. His natural persona could only be described as a "good ol' boy" from rural Tennessee, and he could backslap, eat barbecue with gusto, quote Conway Twitty, and talk trucks with anyone. However, as he rose to executive positions in a major automotive supplier company, he frequently found himself travelling to Detroit.

When he went "up north" he became a different person. His accent disappeared, and he became a measured but direct speaker who was capable of discussing a wide variety of automotive subjects, including unions, management challenges, sophisticated sports cars, Motown music, and upper Midwestern values.

Soon, he was promoted to the position of managing director for all European operations, which included three technical centers and more than a dozen factories. When Mike saw him in Dusseldorf, Germany, he was the picture of an urbane, polished, and sophisticated American who was the antithesis of the ignorant "ugly American." You could easily believe that he'd been raised on the Upper East Side of Manhattan, had studied at the Sorbonne, and was a regular on the Concorde—in reality, none of these things were true.

He charmed the socks off almost everyone in the company's European operations, and he was probably the most successful manager in that position in the firm's history.

Eventually, he returned to the US and left the auto industry to work in a small family business in the rural South. When Mike encountered him in that environment, he had easily moved back to the character that he was when his career first started to blossom: a smart, open, and folksy guy, with that unique and delightful Tennessee twang that the Grand Ole Opry made famous.

Some people might think that Roy was a chameleon, and somehow untrue to his own personality and values. We think that's a shallow and possibly foolish judgment; instead, we think he was someone who had a deep and impressive reservoir of know-how that allowed him to constantly keep tasks and relationships in balance.

If you recall Sun Tzu's admonition in the Introduction of this book, you'll realize that Roy had, indeed, been able to regulate his methods to match the infinite variety of circumstances.

Good leaders need to be able to sense, understand, and act on the social and visual cues that everyone expects from a leader. Great actors know that the entire look and feel of their presentation is what separates an average performer from a great performer. To do this, they immerse themselves in each part, visualizing how their character would dress, speak, and react in complex circumstances. They think about how they will stand, walk, and sit.

Leaders think about this too, because successful leaders are also actors. Whether you loved or hated Ronald Reagan, it's really impossible to suggest that he was an ineffective leader.

THE PLAYBOOK

- Get feedback from people. Ask your friends and colleagues how they view your personal conduct. Is it consistent with your goals? Are your day-to-day actions those that you would admire if someone else behaved as you do?

- Dress for success in different circumstances. If you're not sure about a situation, ask before you head off to a new place or environment. Almost nothing can damage your chances for successfully influencing people more than a clueless appearance.

- If you reach a transition point and begin to feel you are about to cross an ethical or value-based boundary, stop and think about this in more detail. Create a list of pros and cons and see if that clears your thinking. It's very possible that you can find a way, consistent with your values, which will get you the results you seek.

- For value-driven inflection points, we offer a caution: small, incremental violations of your personal standards are easy to fall into and can lead to serious problems if you aren't conscious about your limits. In life, you will certainly find a few value questions that are black and white. Most, though, are gray—and the more influence you have in an organization, the more gray issues you will confront. How gray must something be before it becomes black? Try this simple, direct query: if your planned action would be posted front and center on a viral Internet post, would you still do it?

- In any situation, there are social rules, which are almost never written down. Do you know the cues for your entrances and exits? If you feel awkward in ambiguous or uncertain public circumstances, you'll probably find that these moments occur at transition points, as discussed in Chapter 2.

- You must always be "on," even when you don't want to be. People expect that from you, and it doesn't matter that you are feeling tired, had a bad day, or even have indigestion from what you ate at lunch. If you aren't feeling your best, just imagine you are walking out on stage, about to execute a script and *act out* a role. You might even want to outline the "script" before you meet some, enter a meeting, or start a teleconference.

- Choose your tone with some care. If you find yourself working with hard-boiled male construction workers from New Jersey, they might not respect you if you can't selectively cuss like a dock worker. If you use the same demeanor in Salt Lake City, however, you might find that you are politely but firmly invited to leave as soon as possible. You don't need to get drawn into the "political correctness" debate, but you should consider what's appropriate and what's respectable wherever you go. Crude and coarse language is rarely acceptable, and even when it is, you need you use it with great care.

- When in doubt, be nice to people. This isn't difficult to understand; it's just difficult to do if your inner-alligator has never been tamed. If you habitually fall off the stage in this regard, revisit the Clipboard and Playbook entries in Chapter 5.

- Avoid sarcasm. Unless you are extremely close to everyone within earshot, sarcasm is easily misunderstood. Jokes can also go badly; few of us are professional comedians, and even the most successful comedians occasionally tell a joke that turns out very sour and offends people. It's OK to laugh but think hard before you turn loose.

Behavior 5. Look *out* of the window and *into* the mirror.

Victory has a thousand fathers; defeat is an orphan.

This quote is often attributed to John F. Kennedy in Arthur M. Schlesinger Jr.'s book "The Thousand Days." In point of fact, it was first uttered by Galeazzo Ciano, Benito Mussolini's son-in-law, co-founder of the Italian fascist movement, and Foreign Minister under Mussolini.

No matter, this is still a powerful idea that effective leaders understand. Yes, victory needs to be shared widely, but defeat needs to be openly and honestly confronted and must form the basis for ongoing learning and development.

In "Good to Great," Jim Collins's follow up to "Built to Last," Collins lays out the issues that differentiate average leaders from exceptional leaders. The greatest difference, according to Collins, is the ability to blend "extreme personal humility with intense professional will."

The image Collins developed to illustrate this is that influential people are able to look outward—through a window—and to look inward—at a mirror—to explain this balancing act between modesty and determination.

Great leaders look out the window when credit for success is doled out. In other words, they point to others when things go well.

Conversely, when things didn't go well, they first look in the mirror to assign responsibility. They are willing to be accountable when events turn against them.

Nelson Mandela put it another way: "It is better to lead from behind and to put others in front, especially when you celebrate victory when nice things occur. You take the front line when there is danger. Then people will appreciate your leadership."

Retired US Army General Tom Kolditz, who is Professor Emeritus at the US Military Academy at West Point and is also the founding Director of the Doerr Institute for New Leaders at Rice University offers yet another angle on this idea. In his book, "In Extremis Leadership—Leading As If Your Life Depended On It," Kolditz points out that, in dangerous circumstances, the most successful leaders are those that put their own well-being behind that of their followers.

These men and women also share lifestyles and risks with their followers. They tend to focus outwardly—through Collins' window—on the environment around them and focus less inwardly (into Collin's mirror) toward a personal perspective.

If you can consistently look out of the window and, at the right times, into the mirror, you will find that you'll gain skill and ability in balancing your own self-awareness (Chapter Five) and empathy (Chapter Eight)—two critical leadership aptitudes.

One of Mike's major consulting projects required him to lead a team to carry out a diagnostic study of a major automaker, with operations in several international zones. The study was commissioned by one of the managers in one of the international zones—but that zone was not the "home country" zone. Once Mike's draft of his team findings was presented to the sponsoring executive, Mike knew he had a problem. What the executive really wanted (he'd never hinted at this before) was an account that pointed out how the shortcomings in the home zone led to major problems in this other zone.

There was a great deal of truth in that assertion, but Mike tried to explain that it was vitally important for this executive to clean up his own messes before he could hope to have any real influence with the central authorities in this megafirm. Mike shifted some of the emphasis in his final report to reflect the weight and impact that home country zone missteps had on the other international zones, but he retained a detailed breakdown of problems as well as potential solutions that the sponsoring zone organization should undertake to help themselves.

Several consequences flowed from this. First, Mike was <u>not</u> retained to lead the second phase of the project—the implementation of potential solutions. In other words, he was fired for espousing a reasonable and constructive level of candor. Second, the actual follow-on activities veered away from the suggested plan that Mike and his team had devised, with more emphasis on confrontation with and culpability for the home country zone organization.

A couple of years later, Mike noted in the press that the sponsoring zone organization experienced a major upheaval. The executive team was purged, and new managers were installed. Within two months, a new plan for this business unit was announced. More than 75% of this plan was remarkably close to what Mike and his team had suggested in their final report—some of it was almost verbatim from the report.

Today, seventeen years after this experience, the remaining part of this story can now be told. The company was Volkswagen, and one of the challenges that was included in this consulting study was VW's desire to make Diesel engines the centerpiece of their vehicles.

Although professional confidentiality prevents divulging details, the underlying issue was a set of senior management decisions that literally ignored basic physical laws and demanded a rapid, no-cost way to overcome the inherent limitations of Diesel cycle engines. And this demand was unconditional; it was a "do it or else" sort of thing.

Mike's report advised VW management that they were headed down a very nasty route, and the executive team's non-negotiable insistence was one of the major reasons. A decade later, the convoluted and illegal effort used to evade basic physics was revealed, and the outcome was beyond terrible—$30 billion and counting, plus untold tons of illegal pollution. Nearly everyone who understood the technical issues was utterly stunned by the details of what VW had done, but the earlier behavior of management was the first step down the path that ended so badly.

This story isn't about Mike, his team, and the report. It's simpler: if the original executive team had been willing to look into the mirror, and act on their problems in a constructive manner, this organizational roller coaster ride might have been averted.

There's another side that further illustrates the window and mirror principle. Mike needed to look in the mirror and see why he had missed the cues that caused him to be blissfully unaware of the sponsoring organization's desire to use consultants as a "wedge" to affect the headquarters operation—and to curry favor in Germany via support for the

Diesel initiative. That should have raised some ethical issues early in the engagement, and, had that happened, it could have been dealt with in a more constructive fashion.

THE PLAYBOOK

- Consistently give credit for success to others. If you have regular after-the-fact project reviews, make sure this is something you stress. People will be able to see through insincere praise, so you need to do more than just throw out a few off-the-cuff comments for this to be effective. "Everyone knows how hard Susan has worked on this," might be true and even flattering, but it won't be as effective as highlighting the specific and exceptional things that Susan accomplished.

- After a failure, scrutinize your own actions first. Avoid blaming others, and don't let the idea that you were the victim of events beyond your control invade your assessment. That might be accurate, and it might be helpful to understand the details, but you have to take care of your own failings before you can hope to convince others to do the same.

- Just keep telling yourself it's not all about you. If you have difficulty with this, once again the simplest thing you can do is create a two-column list, similar to the pro-con analysis we've suggested in other Playbook entries. On one side, list the things that went well, and who contributed to these positive outcomes. On the other side, list things that didn't turn out well. However, instead of listing someone to blame, for each entry record what you might have done differently as a leader, knowing what you know now.

- If you find that looking in the mirror is not easy, get someone else to do a diagnostic for you. At times, it's tough or even impossible for anyone who was part of a project to carry out a reasonably objective assessment, particularly for failed undertakings.

Behavior 6. Don't get stuck on the dark side of human intolerance.

In Rob's book "Awakening from the Deep Sleep," he listed 25 examples of ways men can find themselves slumbering in the "deep sleep" of life. These largely were examples of what happens when traditional behaviors hold men back. Rob's book was directed toward men, but the main message has a wider application: Anyone can be hemmed in by the expectations of others or of society as a whole.

Whether it's about gender, race, religious belief and/or ethnicity-based notions, a self-imposed and persistent belief that you are constrained is a self-defeating conviction. We all know that prejudice and hatred remain a subterranean element of the human soul, but leaders must have the courage to fly in the face of these murky attributes.

It's bad enough if you permit the deep-seated xenophobia that lurks inside many of us to affect the way you treat those around you.

Worst of all is allowing the intolerance that others feel to infect and limit your own potential and behavior.

The political environment of the 21st century has brought many of these stereotypes onto national and international stages, and one can only hope that ongoing discussion and self-examination will, sooner or later, move society's sensitivity needle.

This is a particularly important matter when dealing with the most recent generation of technical workers. They've been raised in a society where many of the issues that provoke a visceral, gut-level response in their elders have absolutely no impact on their emotional state. If they see you allowing something in this vein to surface, most of them will lose confidence in you very quickly.

The flip side of the coin is also perceptible in Gen Y and Millennial cohorts. They don't feel constrained to any extent by some of the ideas that have been present in human society for thousands of years. Mike's Millennial daughter Jocelyn was born with an extremely high level of intelligence, and she often drove her parents a bit crazy with her beyond-her-years abilities.

She also exhibited a strong aptitude for mathematics, and, like her father, was drawn to engineering as a profession. While she faced—and still confronts—some degree of prejudice about her role as a female engineer, that hasn't seemed to affect her enjoyment and excitement about her work. It never occurred to her that she shouldn't enter the world of technology because her chromosomes were somehow "wrong." She earned Professional Registration before she reached 30 and is now a successful environmental engineer.

Mike can reflect back to his studies and early career—a time that was only yesterday in the long stream of human history—when having a "girl" in any engineering class was not only unusual, it made everyone wonder about her personality, motives, and (of course) her appearance.

In sum, giving in to chauvinism, bigotry, and other forms of intolerance will cause you to get "stuck" in a place where your leadership capability will be stunted and ultimately deformed.

When you have this burden on your back, whether you are giving or taking from the dark side, it can become impossible to develop, maintain, and exhibit the level of energy, gusto and confidence that people expect from a leader.

THE PLAYBOOK

- Connect with others in a meaningful and respectful manner. If you need to improve on this, try thinking about people in terms of their productive capability. As a technical leader, that matters more than any visual cues you might get from their appearance.

- Don't allow stereotypical thinking to infect your team, even if you have to confront someone about this. Explain that it's OK with you if someone doesn't conform to narrow stereotypes, as long as they are industrious and constructive individuals. If someone exhibits rank prejudice, make sure you counsel them privately about the impact that their behavior can and will have on the tasks that your team must complete.

- If you feel *you* are limited by prejudice, remember Eleanor Roosevelt's famous adage, "Nobody can make you feel inferior without your permission."

- Treat people the way you want to be treated. If you get it wrong, don't hesitate to recognize your error and apologize for your mistake. Apologies in these areas can be the most difficult you will ever undertake but allowing an error to go unacknowledged will almost certainly be counter-productive to your role and effectiveness as a leader.

- Always start with a high opinion of others; it may be the most important thing you can do. An "innocent until proven guilty" standard is a great starting point.

- Consider physician-essayist Lewis Thomas' words: "We are educated to be amazed by the infinite variety of life forms in nature; we are, I believe, only at the beginning of being flabbergasted by its unity."

CHAPTER EIGHT

The Coach's Clipboard: You Can Put Yourself in the Other Guy's Shoes...

Part of being leader is helping *other* people grow and develop. When you do that, you extend your influence, because people will look to you for guidance and advice, and that's one of the most powerful forms of influence you can wield.

However, you really can't hope that you will be able to do much of that unless you are capable of identifying and understanding the emotional reactions of those around you. That means you need to develop your sense of empathy.

Empathy is not the same as sympathy. Empathy is about *recognizing* and *comprehending* the feelings and emotional reactions of others. Sympathy—often used incorrectly as a synonym for empathy—is about *sharing and absorbing* the feelings of others, particularly feelings of sadness, loss, and anguish.

Some people often say "empathy" when they really mean kind-hearted—or even soft-headed. We don't think that necessarily applies to what you need to do to be more effective as a leader. What we do think is important is that you can appreciate when people are up, when they're down, when they need a pat on the back, and, at times, when they need a boot in the rear.

To be a Fourth Wave leader, you need to be able to look, observe, listen and absorb the moods, joys, and unhappy reactions of the people you want to influence. If you can't, you're likely to default to an all-tasks and no-relationship approach to work, a reaction that, over time, will diminish your individual significance and influence.

Behavior 1. Read the emotional cues that others transmit.

There are a number of serious scientific studies of empathy, and some of the most interesting findings are related to how and why yawning is contagious. We all know that once one person in a group starts to yawn, others who are present are more apt to start yawning as well.

One of the major findings is that people who yawn more frequently in response to someone else yawning are more likely to have higher levels of empathy than those who contagiously yawn less often. Catriona Morrison, at the University of Leeds in the UK, has done a great deal of work in this area, and her results, supported by research completed by Dr Atsushi Senju of Birkbeck College, University of London show that yawning and empathetic emotions both activate the precuneus and posterior temporal gyrus areas in the brain.

In a study presented at the British Association Festival of Science in 2007, Morrison compared the yawning and empathetic reactions of a relatively large group of psychologists and engineers. (Rob and Mike find this particularly interesting!) She found that psychologists contagiously yawned four or five times as often as engineers, and that engineers consistently scored lower on perceptual evaluations that reflect empathetic reactions.

Interestingly, she also found no statistically significant difference between men and women in either contagious yawning or empathetic reactions—just differences between psychologists and engineers.

This work was both presaged by a study at Drexel University in Philadelphia by a team led by Steven Platek. After testing a group of individuals for their ability to respond to the mental stress others were feeling in difficult circumstances, they then allow these same individuals to observe people who, at various times, yawned, through a one-way mirror.

Those who were best able to read and react to the stress of others also yawned substantially more after seeing someone else yawn.

One of Morrison's ideas is particularly relevant, though: "The theory is we yawn contagiously to show empathy and the evolutionary explanation is it is a warning to the group that we need to be more alert." Morrison also believes that psychologists, trained and conditioned to observe and probe deeply into the human psyche, are more likely to "have more social awareness."

Conversely, engineers are more likely to be interested, trained, and skilled in taking devices apart, looking at mechanisms, circuit diagrams, complex computer code, and, in general, are more comfortable and able to read *things* more acutely than they can read people.

We think this is a critical area for engineers and technologists who want to exercise leadership. Tech heads need to recognize that this is a skill worth developing and is vitally important to organizational survival. We may no longer need to be wary of saber tooth tigers, but we do need to be aware and react appropriately when others perceive risk, danger, or, on the flip side, opportunity and potential.

An effective way to develop your empathetic ability is to foster team spirit. Draw out those you work with and learn about who they are as people, what they're about, what interests they have besides work, what their family histories are. Take the time to get to know them.

The objective is to get everyone to understand each other's goals and dreams beyond work and to get people to talk to each other. Team members inevitably draw closer as a result of these kinds of discussions. They learn to build each other up, not drag each other down.

THE PLAYBOOK

- Make time in meetings for social interaction. No meeting should ever be held without an agenda, but the best agendas either have specific time at the beginning of the meeting for informal discussion, enough slack time to permit people to interact in ways that are not purely task related—that permit or even encourage relationship development.

- Meetings are about accomplishing tasks, but a great deal of important communication occurs informally. Carefully observe others in your next meeting (don't stare, though). Try and see what their body language is saying, how they sit up, slump, or lean in their chairs. Watch what people are doing with their hands. Study after study shows that somewhere between 60 and 90% of the information that's transmitted in face-to-face communication is contained in non-verbal cues rather than verbal information.

- Learn to shift gears when the terrain changes. If you're going uphill, you may need to gear down. When you've got a tailwind, you might be able to cruise in overdrive. This is yet another example of how transition points often trip up technical people. Many engineers can picture this: you've been engaged in a complex and intricate analysis, possibly during a meeting with other tech heads. Suddenly, you're summoned to an executive's office to answer questions about some crisis. Your instinctive response is to start talking about the most technical aspects of the problem, and yet the executive wants to learn general facts and your overall impression. You start on a detailed and well-thought out explanation of the underlying methodological issues, and the executive starts to think, "What a dweeb—I don't want to get into all of this." If this happens, you'll be able to see it in the exec's face and body language. Shift gears and think about what the executive wants to know, not what you want to say.

- Try and learn about the visions that your friends and family have about the future. They have dreams, too, and you might find synergy with your professional goals in these areas. After all, the supporting relationships that you develop away from your career are an important element in the task-relationship balance that will make you a better leader, a better partner, a better parent, and a better citizen. You may have to ask searching questions to draw out these dreams, but it can be worth more than you might guess.

Behavior 2. Improve your empathy skills by overcoming instinctive responses.

Every human being has a powerful survival instinct. If you don't have a strong desire for life and a reflexive approach to the world around you, you won't have to worry too much about your leadership skills and abilities. This may be particularly true during a serious pandemic.

Survival comes from deep within our brain structure—it's a huge aspect of the behaviors that are guided by the R-complex and limbic system. Whenever you are threatened, almost everyone will feel an immediate need to respond in an active way. You're not likely to observe and try and assess the situation in a measured and thoughtful way; instead, you do something, often the first thing that pops into your head.

If you didn't feel that way, you might not make it through the day. If you're driving on a freeway, and someone cuts you off, you don't stop and try to define the problem, analyze the other driver's psyche, and then determine a root cause. You respond, quickly and, we hope, effectively. You might offer the offending driver a snappy hand signal as well, but almost none of your reaction is thought out and considered.

This is a tendency that interferes with problem solving and specifically obstructs your ability to develop empathetic responses in the workplace. Most people reading this book have likely had some type of formal problem solving training. The steps are the same, no matter what the technique is called. You start by carefully defining what should have happened and compare the desired outcome to the actual situation—and the difference is some sort of gap. Then, you try to determine root causes for the gap. Then and only then do you consider possible solutions.

If you watch people actually try and solve problems, though, what you see is a far cry from this measured and considered approach. Instead, solutions fly as fast as anyone can spit them out. "Oh, I know what's wrong. Do 'x' and the problem will go away." Little careful thought, and no application of that expensive problem-solving training, just jump right in and throw out fixes.

And, we all know what comes from that approach. Problem resolution efforts are abysmal in most organizations. Less than one in five problems are ever completely solved, even when formal teams are convened to work on a problem. Although some reduction of the magnitude and impact of a problem occurs in many cases, in an alarmingly large number of instances, formal problem-solving efforts actually make things worse, not better.

Dare we say this pattern played out in the early stages of the COVID-19 pandemic?

This is a direct result of the instinctive and reflexive response most everyone has to troubles. Presumably, your DNA lineage is still active because, one afternoon on the savannah, one of your distant relatives saw a lion—and immediately took steps to improve his or her chances of survival. They didn't stop and consider whether the lion was hungry, or whether this might be a chance to permanently prevent lion attacks in the future, they just responded instinctively.

The same thing is true in the way many people respond to the emotional states of others, and there's nothing more fundamental to developing a strong empathetic capability than developing better skill in listening and understanding what other people are trying to tell you.

One of Steven Covey's "Seven Habits of Highly Effective People" is to seek first to understand and then to be understood. As Covey points out, most of us listen with the immediate intent to reply, just as we tend to exclaim we know the solution to a problem without careful reflection of the nature of the problem. We are so full of ourselves we often don't allow the emotional state of another to influence our thinking. This causes people to evaluate, probe, interpret, and advise rather than truly understanding others.

These responses are, like fleeing from a lion, instinctive and reflexive. For many people, though, they aren't very empathetic. Instead, they are the impatient responses of someone who is predominantly task-oriented—and, without really thinking about it and certainly without intending to be—dismissive of what other people think and say.

To improve your behavior in this area, you might find that you will be better served by developing specific practices that address your impatience. These can be tiny habits or big ones, sprinkled throughout the day as a way to stop and reconnect, if only for a moment.

THE PLAYBOOK

- When listening to someone else speak and hear a useful idea, write it down. Later, you may want to restate this in a way that makes sense for you—but at the time you hear it, simply try and record what you have heard. If you start to process the idea in detail, you will fall into the evaluate-probe-interpret-advise loop that blocks real comprehension.

- Be aware of the drama of everyday life and alert to the surprises that will appear before you as surely as the sun rises and sets. Don't worry if there's a bit of silence after someone speaks; it may be that there's more to be said—but only if you are willing to keep silent and let someone else have the floor.

- In any encounter, search for what you can learn, enjoy and appreciate from another. How can you do this? The simplest, easiest way is to ask the other person to explain in more detail. Another possibility is to admit that you didn't fully understand what was said and ask the person who was speaking to explain the idea again.

- If you feel that you are not letting others express their ideas before you jump in, you may benefit from paying some attention to your breathing while others are speaking. When your reflexive responses seem to "jump" out of your throat, inhale. Only skilled ventriloquists and a few world-class reed musicians are able to speak when they are breathing in.

- Avoid being the first person to offer an opinion in a meeting or even in a one-on-one encounter. You may be tempted to do so, but you will probably get more out of meetings if you allow others to speak first. This is even more powerful when you have formal authority—when you are the boss of others present. If you speak first, they will conclude, "That's what she (or he) wants, no reason to buck the system, it's OK by me, if it goes wrong, it's not my fault," and so forth. And, see if others will take a stand before you add your opinion. An early endorsement is almost the same as offering your opinion first, while an early critique will discourage others from offering an additional opinion that you might belittle.

- To increase your influence, it is usually better to wait, hear from others, understand what they are saying, and then add your ideas and observations. This is the mark of a deep thinker and can help you develop a new and more powerful empathetic behaviors.

Behavior 3. Fill those buckets.

Authors Tom Rath and Donald O. Clifton used research by the Gallup Organization and their own interviews to craft the bestseller "How Full Is Your Bucket?"

The picture that Rath and Clifton paint is a simple one. You start out every day with a bucket and a dipper. As the day progresses, you can fill other people's buckets by dipping into your own and saying something positive, showing interest, or simply asking how a project, assignment, or other activity is progressing.

You empty your bucket by saying positive things. But you can also dump your bucket on someone's head—which is not what you want to do.

The other side of the bucket story is that this process is contagious. If you fill the buckets of your associates, family and friends with positive things, they are much more likely to return the favor and add water to *your* bucket.

This isn't complicated: if you work for me and I build you up, you're more likely to develop and mentor the people who work for you and with you. That makes everyone more productive, and probably happier. If I dump on you, you're more likely to dump on peers and subordinates, which will reduce productivity and make every feel like they're trapped in Dilbert World.

In the first two decades of the 21st century, the importance of the bucket analogy is increasing.

Jean M. Twenge, whose book "Generation Me: Why Today's Young Americans Are More Confident, Assertive, Entitled—and More Miserable Than Ever Before," summarizes a great deal of what is known about the post Gen X workforce, is engaged in an ongoing and substantial study of how people respond to workplace norms and behaviors.

With co-author Stacy Campbell, Twenge, a professor at San Diego State University, has reviewed approximately 1.4

million personality attitude surveys, behavior scale instruments, and aptitude tests completed by people and dating back to the 1930's. The conclusions of this massive study are probably unsurprising to most Millennials but might be jarring to the Gen X'ers and Baby Boomers who are largely responsible for supervising and mentoring these maturing leaders.

Both Millennials and the emerging Gen-Y group entering the workforce in the US have extremely high levels of self-esteem—they are confident and, as a rule, have a relatively low need for the approval of others. In other words, they are, more often than not, sure of themselves, and don't particularly feel that they need to be nurtured. They are also more self-absorbed than ever before and are convinced that their very existence will change the way society works.

Beyond these feelings, these two generational groups are also given to a high level of anxiety and depression, which is probably not surprising given the combination of narcissism and self-confidence that Twenge and Campbell uncovered.

As Twitter, Instagram, and other social network tools have become the next evolution of broadcasted instant communication, the implications of ever-increasing stream-of-consciousness interaction is almost indisputable. The workplace is now more connected and more village-like even as globalization ebbs and spreads.

Everyone knows more about everyone else. And, given the human penchant for gossip, bad news spreads faster than good news in a Tweeting society—as do malicious, deceptive, and disruptive ideas.

For leaders, the implication is extraordinary. If you fill one person's bucket, this news will spread slowly. If you dump your bucket on someone, dozens, hundreds, or thousands of people may know within minutes.

Fill those buckets—and don't dump them, ever!

Mike likes to joke that, if you need to dump a bucket on someone, hire a consultant. After all, they'll be gone as soon as they get paid and you can blame it on them if things turn sour later…

THE PLAYBOOK

- People remember and respect those who make them feel special. If you can't show appreciation, people won't stick around. Try to find an opportunity to demonstrate your appreciation for someone else at least once a week, more often if you can do it without being insincere or patronizing. So, be genuine about your praise. Don't heap it on for the sake of appearances—people are savvy about this sort of thing and will see through it in a New York minute.

- Keep track of the abundances of your day—the times when someone has been nice to you or when you've done someone a favor, when a meeting has gone particularly well or when you've offered someone praise or encouragement. Jot them down on your I-Phone or in a notepad in your purse. Research by psychologist John Gottman shows that healthy relationships have a ratio of <u>five positive interactions for every negative one</u>. If you have a particularly important or difficult person you work with on a regular basis, see what your ratio of dips to dumps might be.

- The bucket theory is all about building self-esteem in those around you. So if you are handing out more corrections than pats on the back, people are going to start feeling bad about themselves. Every time you come in the room, they're going to want to duck under their desks or chairs, whether it's your employees or your kids. If you want to be a star on the web, let your anger or displeasure get the best of you.

- Be specific about what you praise. Draw attention to a report or a comment made in a meeting. And remember, nothing that we can buy someone gives as much happiness as the gift of our awareness and ultimately, our approbation or approval. The easiest way to do this is to smile.

- Sometimes you can make a positive out of a negative. If you notice someone seems out of sorts or is struggling, ask what's wrong. Find out what kind of help they need or whether they have the resources to get the job done. As a manager, this is a powerful way to avoid falling into the micromanager trap; view your role as "roadblock remover" rather than "surrogate doer."

- Keep track of your own achievements every day. Nine out of 10 people say they're more productive when they're around positive people, so be an example of what you want others to be like. You really have only three choices when you respond to others: praise, ignore or criticize. When we fill another's bucket, we automatically fill our own.

Behavior 4. Use the strengths of those around you to keep teams in balance.

A great team will have plenty of balance. In sports, that usually means a number of real stars, supported by "role players" who make the stars even better. In the best teams, the stars also make the role players perform better, too. Finally, wherever a truly exceptional championship team can be found, you will also hear talk about people who are "good in the locker room."

What does this really mean? To some extent, there's a bit of cause-and-effect confusion afoot. Teams that do well—teams that win—are almost always happier than teams that do poorly or lose more often than they win. Does happiness cause winning—or does winning cause happiness?

Casey Stengel, who managed the New York Yankees baseball team for 12 seasons, from 1949 to 1960 and won seven World Series championships (and lost in the Series twice) in that time span, always knew that talent alone wasn't the key to winning.

Talent is necessary; Stengel managed in the major leagues for 25 years, and never won a championship with the other teams he managed. In fact, his New York Mets team of 1962 still holds the record for the most losses in a single season (120) of any professional sports team.

But even when you have great talent, leadership plays a key role. As Stengel once said, "The secret of managing is to keep the guys who hate you away from the guys who are undecided."

This really tells us a great deal about building successful work teams.

First, you shouldn't expect to be loved. Remember, a belief that everyone ought to love you is one of the irrational thoughts that are counter-productive.

Second, you need to understand how those who work with you are likely to respond in various circumstances. That doesn't mean you should accept stereotypes about other people—most human beings we've ever met have some qualities that are consistent with a stereotype but also a significant number of traits that don't match up with the pigeonhole they appear to fit. Almost everyone is deeper than a simple label.

Third, you need to understand and make use of the personalities that you have to work with. To do this, you need to recognize and understand that almost everyone has a general personality type. And, once you can distinguish who is more likely to exhibit a given set of personality traits, you can make use of their strengths more effectively.

If you can achieve this as a leader, you are much more likely to build a strong base of relationships and to improve your ability to accomplish tasks. However, you also need to be aware of—and guard against—the negative elements of personality that all of us have.

Psychologists recognize four basic personality types:

- **Competitive:** Every activity or project is a contest and these people are driven to win. There's a strong focus on tasks for competitive individuals. That's positive, but it's also something that can get out of hand and turn destructive if ethical or legal boundaries are crossed.
- **Collaborative:** These are the peacemakers; everything's an opportunity to build relationships.

This helps cement a group together, but, if leadership doesn't watch out, a team dominated by collaborative people will spend all their time drinking coffee or tea, talking about the latest YouTube video, and otherwise having a good time, and won't get much done.

- **Creative:** They're the innovators; everything's an opportunity to innovate, invent, and craft something new and exciting. Creative types are also full of energy, and this can be quite positive for a team. At some point in every project, though, the creativity needs to end and execution needs to begin. Some creative individuals want to tinker with a product, a project, or an idea forever.

- **Consistent:** They like order and routine; every situation is an opportunity to plan and improve order. That's a true strength in today's working environment, but as rapidly as the world changes these days, it can also be a crippling deficiency. What worked in the last project may work again this time, but processes need constant updating and continual improvement to remain effective. If someone seems peeved when necessary changes are made, that's an indication that they're driven—or possibly obsessed--by consistency.

One type isn't better than another, merely different. Most of us are a combination of two of these types and we may share some of the characteristics of a third. Nevertheless, almost everyone has a dominant side that's reflected in one of these archetypes, and a good leader will keep that in mind when delegating and working with people.

So, for example, if you have a project for a game-changing new product, you will need to generate new ideas. If you give this assignment to someone who loves detail and order, you might not get the outcome that you need. The resulting plan probably won't be free-wheeling enough to open the creative floodgates.

As the project progresses, you might find that the overall responsibility will need to shift from a creative individual to a detail-oriented person who excels when consistency is called for.

We often hear managers and executives argue about how teams should be organized. Some say you need a strong project manager; others claim this is a waste of money and you should rotate leaders as projects move along. Still others believe that a particular skill position—say, a design engineer in a product development group—should always lead.

In watching this for many years, our conclusion is more complex: all of these views are right, and all of them are wrong. It all depends on the nature of the project, and if you always assign leadership roles the same way, you're likely to be wrong—sometimes terribly wrong—at least some of the time.

The bottom line is simple: you have to read and understand the key strengths and weaknesses of those around you to be a truly effective leader. All of these personality types are needed for day-in and day-out success, but it's how you deploy people in the context of a project or assignment that matters.

THE PLAYBOOK

- Know the personality types on your team and strive for diversity and balance. However, you won't always get a perfect mix, nor should you expect that you will. One of the best ways to approach this, however, is to hire for attitude and train for skill, which is the opposite of what most people do. Hiring a jerk—or someone whose personality type is clearly at odds with the tasks in front of you—won't be helpful no matter what skill level they can bring to the table.

■ The way an individual approaches their work can reflect on their personality. This can help you identify and make the best use of everyone's skills and character traits. Here are some the broad outlines of what you should look for in understanding the strengths of your teammates:

1. Collaborators need a sense of team play, and revel in a supportive family-like environment. They genuinely enjoy company social events, and are often the ones who organize lunches, after-work events, and similar non-task activities. Their response to difficult times is to pull everyone together to share feelings of stress and worry.

2. Competitors need tough opponents, so big challenges get them excited and bring out their best efforts. When things are bleak, they become energized.

3. Consistent people need to keep a schedule. The "same time, same place" mentality is obvious, as is their irritation when things get unpredictable. When times are tough, they can retreat into a shell, hoping that the safety of repetitive work will bring an end to the stress they feel.

4. For creative types, the world is their playground. They careen from idea to idea, sometimes scoring impressive gains, and sometimes missing the mark by a wide margin. When routine is called for, they exhibit boredom and, in some cases, rebel against the rules. They may be oblivious to external stress factors such as difficult economic times or a competitive business threat.

- Opposites are prone to conflict, competitive types clash with collaborative types, and creative types with consistent types. This can make diverse personalities an asset or a liability, depending on the circumstances. Make assignments and delegate tasks with this in mind.

- As projects become more complex, a great leader will try and hire or assign work to managers who have a collaborative bent. You can teach technical skills, but it can take years to teach empathy for customers or fellow employees.

Behavior 5. Credit's like fertilizer—spread it around and watch things grow.

One of Rob's clients, Richard Sheridan, runs Menlo Innovations, a computer software development firm that has won awards for its flexible workplace concept. (Sheridan's title is "CEO & Chief Storyteller.") Sheridan's team is built around pairs of programmers and developers. Every week, the pairs are swapped and everyone is always working with someone else. This attacks a common problem in software development, where code is so tied to one person, it's tough for anyone else to understand it or work with it.

Sheridan's idea has another major benefit: if you have diversity of ideas in any project, you'll increase the intellectual get-up-and-go applied to the venture. People also will catch each other's mistakes more easily. And they'll continually look at the project with fresh eyes. In Sheridan's shop, it's not that no one gets the credit; instead, credit is shared, and criticism is supportive rather than disruptive.

This approach makes a great deal of sense. Unfortunately, it's far from the norm.

If you spend time with a wide variety of professional and technical people in the workplace, as Mike and Rob have done, you are struck by four recurring themes. These ideas are certainly not universal, but they arise with such consistency that there's something important going on in organizations that leaders need to understand.

1. People are unclear about what they are supposed to do on a day-to-day basis.
2. People feel they are given conflicting direction, and then are asked to sort out the priorities on their own.
3. When things go wrong, you find out as the problem surfaces, often as soon as it becomes apparent.
4. When things go right, you almost never hear anything.

To some extent, these reactions are symptomatic of poor organizations. But we think they reveal another side of organizational life that's often ignored. Managers don't like to complement people when they've done a good job—some managers have come to believe that acknowledging good performance, even outstanding performance, is risky and counter-productive.

How can that possibly be true?

In a seminal article in *Fast Company* in August 2005, Keith H. Hammonds laid out a simple premise: people hate the human resources function in most companies. Hammonds cites a number of reasons, which include:

- HR people don't know much about finance, so they are rarely keyed into the bona fide driving forces in a business.

- Human resource departments prefer to measure efficiency rather than value, because it provides numbers that appear meaningful—but rarely are. It's easier to measure how someone scores on a post-seminar test than it is to measure whether or not the training experience improved someone's on-the-job performance.

- HR's real job—in far too many companies—consists of *protecting the company from the employees;* this means preventing employment lawsuits, bad publicity, and regulatory rebukes for things like Equal Employment Opportunity; Occupational Safety and Health issues; age, sex, race, and religious discrimination; prejudicial discharge; and many other nuances of employment law and regulation.

As Hammonds notes,

> "Human-resources departments benchmark salaries, function by function and job by job, against industry standards, keeping pay—even that of the stars—within a narrow band determined by competitors. They bounce performance appraisals back to managers who rate their employees too highly, unwilling to acknowledge

accomplishments that would merit much more than the 4% companywide increase."[4]

Mike even met one engineering supervisor who claimed that his company issued a mandate: on a 5-point evaluation scale, and with 10 categories for evaluation, every employee—every single one—had to have a final average score between 3.2 and 3.6. He had been told that this was policy because pay raises had to be tied to performance reviews, and no one could get a raise that was more than 3% or less than 2% on an annual basis.

In this kind of environment, supervisors and managers soon learn that praising anyone's work can get you into trouble. When performance reviews are due, and one of your reports recalls the compliment she received for some great work she did on a particular project, she is likely to have a hard time accepting an average rating.

This through-the-looking glass world view eventually ends up confusing everyone about what is, and what isn't sound performance.

When in doubt, fill the buckets! If you find that you are under pressure from a counter-productive review system, you may need to do what all great leaders need to do from time to time. You can accept that bad rules will cause you to perform badly, or you can choose to work around bad rules and maybe, just maybe, be more effective. Of course, if you're caught, you may be chastised (or worse) for breaking

---

[4] Hammonds' article has drawn a great deal of attention over the years. An interesting—and possibly valid—critique of Hammonds' article can be found at https://upstarthr.com/wp-content/uploads/2010/05/Why_We_Hate_HR_Teaching_Guide_FINAL_4-06.pdf. Nevertheless, many of Hammonds' conclusions still apply in 2020.

the rules, but you are likely to end up failing—and suffering similar consequences as you might if you evade the system—if you follow the bad rules.

No one ever said that being a Fourth Wave leader was easy.

THE PLAYBOOK

- Try Sheridan's approach and mix up the composition of the teams periodically—rotate assignments and build wider skills and capabilities for everyone. This will increase your team's overall capability, keep people interested, and create a strong learning environment.
- Give credit to the team, not to any single team leader or member. Post positive comments on-line or conspicuously in your workspace documenting team successes—just make sure that your information is sound and based on facts, not internal PR or spin. You can even post photos of teams that have done noteworthy things.
- Avoid blaming one person for a failure or setback. It's the team's responsibility, win or lose. When things go wrong, never ask "who goofed?" Instead, ask about the underlying process and activities that went astray, and make sure you build a better process or system for the next round.
- Send personal notes congratulating friends on their successes. This can—and should—extend beyond the immediate chain of command that you are part of. Building a network of friends and colleagues beyond your team is the mark of a budding leader.
- If you find you feel constrained by a crazy performance review system, don't hesitate to tell

people when they've done something that's praiseworthy. But do it when you catch them succeeding; don't save it for the quarterly, semi-annual, or annual review process. When performance reviews are due, you may simply have to admit that you are constrained by the review process. Don't go into details unless the rules are readily available to all employees, but an honest discussion of performance should never be a surprise in any event. Even in a bad system, a sound performance review should never bring out things that haven't been discussed in daily activities.

Behavior 6. Help yourself by helping others.

Rob and his wife Pat have a favorite quote from Thomas Mann that is framed in their bedroom:

> *Don't walk behind me, I may not want to lead.*
> *Don't walk before me, I may not want to follow.*
> *Walk by my side and let us be friends.*

For Rob and Pat, this symbolizes the partnership aspect of their marriage. But in this fast-changing world, there's a powerful underlying message for everyone: We are all in this together. To take it a step further, it becomes even more important for us to bring our needs and wants into alignment–side by side–during unsettled times.

In too many organizations, the level of internal competition is greater and more vicious than the competition the firm faces in the marketplace. Why should this be the case?

The logic that arises is simple: "If I do what's best for me, then the organization will get the most from me and it will benefit, too."

The alternative logic—if I do what's best for the company, then I'll benefit, too—is less appealing. And this is less attractive (and even flat-out untrue) for a simple reason: too many managers, and too many companies, don't keep this 'bargain' or compact.

When times are good, the rewards and excitement tend to float upward in the hierarchy, and in bad times, the weight and onus of failure tends to flow rapidly downward. This is reminiscent of the two rules of plumbing:

1. Water seeks its own level.
2. Solids (we know what that constitutes in a plumbing system) run downhill.

Is this an inevitable outcome, or is it just the dark side of human nature? It doesn't have to be this way. There are more constructive and successful ways to lead organizations.

One of Mike's long-term clients was a small Ohio company called the EBO Group. EBO Group started with one business, Power Transmission Technologies, or PT Tech. Founded in 1978, PT Tech's senior leader, Dave Heidenreich (it's not really correct to think of Dave as a CEO or any other typical title—although his nominal position was Chairman), always followed the basic principle that a company that shares with its employees is a company that will prosper.

In 1984, when there were only six employees, PT Tech adopted the "EBO" principle. EBO, which stands for "Excellence By Objective," became the mantra of the business. Everyone knew what the goals were, and the common ground for everyone was clear. If we succeed, we all succeed. If we fail, we all fail.

Then, in 1990, PT Tech started an Employee Stock Ownership Program, or ESOP. This wasn't a phantom stock plan or some other mirage that some ESOP programs use; it was a real and complete transfer of ownership from Heidenreich and the other founders to everyone in the organization. Slowly, as the real meaning of this ownership format took hold, PT Tech grew and prospered. In good times and mostly during bad times, sales and margins grew, as PT Tech's portfolio of heavy industrial brakes and clutches expanded.

By 2002, the ESOP started a new business, called TransMotion Medical, a firm that built sophisticated and innovative mobile chairs and stretchers used in complex medical procedures including endoscopies, mammograms, radiology, and even plastic surgery.

Not long afterward, the ESOP again expanded, starting another new business called IPESsol, which develops and markets innovative photo-voltaic products for renewable energy. The IPESsol project then led to the formation of yet another company, Triton Hybrid Drives, which made use of know-how in the original PT Tech business and the development work done in IPESsol.

While all of this was going forward, the ESOP adopted a new name, The EBO (Excellence By Owners) Group. Through this impressive development phase, EBO continued to grow and earn a profit for the employees.

EBO Group was the kind of company that most people (particularly engineers) dream about working for. It's wasn't perfect; they have troubles and difficulties like any business; the 2002 venture into medical chairs was a result of problems that beset the core business during the 2000-2001 recession. However, the new business development activities required a huge amount of time, energy, and support—and everyone pitched in, working their "normal" job in the older businesses while working extra time every day so that the new businesses could grow and prosper.

It was essentially a non-stop entrepreneurial engine, and it continued to expand and prosper with every new venture. What was the underlying reason for their success?

In effect, the organization had an overt and direct agreement with every employee: you will work for the company, in a structured and defined way, with specific goals and objectives. In return, you will be fairly compensated and will share in the fruits of success. There are few secrets; as owners, everyone has access to the information and news (both good and bad) that drives the business. And the contract is never breached by the company, and only rarely by an employee.

This requires everyone to accept accountability, to demonstrate agility and flexibility to solve problems, to display and practice integrity and honesty at all times, and do this with a passion for excellence so tangible you could taste it when you spent time with the EBO Group's people.

This was done with a simple format everyone completed quarterly. This wasn't an HR driven performance review; instead, it was a dynamic list of things that the company needed from each employee—and it also provided an opportunity for each employee to propose and complete activities that he or she might want to do to further the organization's growth and success.

In short, this was a supportive partnership—a partnership with dozens of equals. And, the lesson for everyone was simple. If you make a deal with most people, and the deal is fair for everyone, you can accomplish things you wouldn't believe possible.

The key factor is that all parties must uphold their end of the bargain. In effect, you help yourself by helping others.

Unfortunately, particularly for those who were part of the EBO Group, when Heidenreich moved away from the core business to focus on the IPESsol venture, things changed. What occurred isn't something that can be shared in detail, but it was clear that the bargain was somehow damaged between management and employees. If the reviews on Glassdoor are any indication, the dynamic that powered the EBO Group no longer operates the way it did for over twenty years.

There are certainly lessons here for technical leaders. First, while few can re-structure their business, let alone create what evolved at the EBO Group, you *can* apply many of the same principles to increase the way your team performs.

Second, the importance of leadership is both fundamental and critical. A positive culture with strong leadership can quickly change if the values and beliefs that made up that culture are not continually supported, nourished, and reinforced.

Third, the EBO Group is still an ongoing business. They may yet recapture what helped them grow for many years, but once trust is broken, it becomes much harder to re-establish trust. Like all business stories, this is an evolving tale and sound leadership is always important.

THE PLAYBOOK

- To the extent that your company will permit, share as much information with everyone as often as possible. Post this in a visible public place and keep it up-to-date. If your company is secretive and tends to conceal important information, find out why and see if you can influence those more senior than you to let loose a bit more.

- If rumors start, make sure you find out what is and isn't known, and try to keep everyone focused on what they can realistically affect. And then emphasize that you can only do what you can do—you can't change things that are beyond your control. As Mike learned from several engineers at General Motors in the period just prior to their bankruptcy, if some of the people working at GM had spent as much time worrying about the work they were supposed to do as they spent worrying about their jobs, they wouldn't have had to worry about their jobs every day.

- Reconsider the way you approach your role as a technical leader. In today's hypercompetitive world, everyone has more work than they can do. Make sure that some of your time is set aside for purposeful leadership activities—explaining policies, communicating the company's status, dealing with rumors, and developing and coaching people. When you look at your overloaded schedule, make sure that these activities—which many people see as "nice but not necessary" don't get squeezed off the agenda.

- When you start a new project, make sure everyone knows the overall goals. If you aren't sure, don't hesitate to say so—far better for everyone to know that there's uncertainty ahead than to think there's a secret plan that they can't know about. Then help the team help break down the goals into achievable tasks. This will build team ownership of the goals, as well as the effort (and likely sacrifices) needed to achieve planned results.

Behavior 7. Give to others and expect nothing in return.

Small children can be and often are extremely self-centered. "Me" is one of the words that toddlers love to throw around. Of course, this makes good sense; a small child's brain hasn't developed, and the view that the world revolves around its very existence is not only normal, but a necessary survival instinct.

Once a child reaches the age of five or so, most kids start to realize their existence occurs in a larger context. More people, more complexity, and more uncertainty start to appear in life, and that usually results in a dim but obvious realization that emotions and feelings aren't completely determined by what other people say or do. Instead, most elementary school kids slowly but surely begin to understand that the way they feel is their own doing. Certainly, outside events and people can and should influence emotions, but final control rests with each individual.

Some children make this transition from a self-centered to a *decentered* view of things quite well, but others do so poorly. A few never make the transition at all. However, the degree of transition does seem to have an impact on the future raw leadership potential a young child might have.

Being somewhat self-centered appears to be healthy and positive. If you can't believe in yourself, then it's unlikely that others will trust in your abilities, either. Being extremely self-centered, though, leaves an egocentric persona that, in an adult, can be perceived as being forceful, farsighted, risk-prone, charismatic, rule-averse, and even coldblooded.

Exceedingly self-centered people are often characterized as narcissists. In Greek mythology, Narcissus was a beautiful young man who became so enamored of his own reflection in a stream that he forgot to drink and died from thirst. "Narcissism" and self-love are often used synonymously.

Some degree of narcissism is positive and helpful, and, over time, psychologists have come to recognize that the range of narcissistic behavior is broad. Narcissism isn't some form of brain disease as much as it is an element of character that varies from person to person.

Many powerful and successful men (in particular) are far along in the spectrum of narcissism. Larry Ellison, the outsized genius behind Oracle, was described in an unauthorized biography as being different from God only because "God doesn't believe he is Larry Ellison."

In short, highly self-centered people are often the perfect representation of heroic, cult-of-personality leadership. This can be particularly true during times of duress or crisis, when many people yearn for dynamic guidance that makes the world seem simple and safe, even when it may not be that way.

Being a poor listener—being unable to put aside your own thoughts and hear what others are trying to tell you—is one symptom of self-centered behavior. Another variant of poor listening is an inability to identify with the feelings and moods of those around you. In essence, a self-absorbed individual doesn't have the 'bandwidth' to sense and understand what others may be feeling, because he or she is too busy with their own emotional state.

Finally, someone who is overly self-centered will be driven to win. This means they are prone to step over the boundaries of integrity and legality, often because they believe that the rules are for others, not for them. This can be a powerful attribute at the right time and right place, but can also, if left unchecked, constitute a fatal flaw that can destroy not only a career but the jobs and livelihoods of many others.

Now, it's important to say again that some degree of self-centered behavior can be a potent tool for success as a leader. You can't take every criticism to heart or hear every word of every dissenter. You don't have to be the world's greatest mentor to be a balanced leader, and you can't be so rigid in your personal integrity that you miss opportunities that are actually ethical and legal. And you do need a passion to win.

If you have a propensity to go a bit far in this direction—and we emphasize again that many influential leaders have some narcissistic tendencies—then you may need a new mantra. A simple yet effective statement of principle is that *you should give and expect nothing in return*. This can free you from the hypersensitivity, egoism, and ethical minefields that self-centered leaders tend to fall into.

The ironic reality is that, if you can learn to give selflessly, you will, by and large, find that you are paid back many times over for your generosity and gracious acts.

Who really knows why some people are successful and others are not? In certain times and places, we find that many different approaches can be successful, again echoing Sun-Tzu's observations about circumstances. In some eras, ruthless self-centered methods work well. In others, selfless sacrifice may prevail.

We believe, though, in the unbalanced and technologically driven times that have punctuated the last few decades, successful technical leaders have, to a large degree, behaved in a more decentered, emotionally intelligent manner. And we also believe that is the way the future will unfold as well.

Regardless of the historical flow, those who find success, whether by accident of birth or by their own hard work, fully distinguish themselves by giving back to the communities and societies from which they arise. To be remembered, to leave footprints that inspire admiration, entails an interest and commitment to something greater than oneself.

As Winston Churchill (who could be more than a bit of a narcissist at times) said, "You make a living by what you get, but you make a life by what you give."

THE PLAYBOOK

- If you find you are given to dismissive responses when others voice opinions, step back and try to detach yourself from the situation. What are the objective facts? Before you respond, consider what you would be willing to publish in an arena where open feedback and criticism of your ideas would be fair game for people you don't know?

- If you find that rage wells inside when others disagree, review Chapter 6 and see if that can quell the ego-beast in you. If that doesn't work, you may want to seek professional assistance. However, we do need to state this clearly: individuals who have a strong self-centered nature are unusually reluctant to seek or accept assistance from anyone. If you are frequently beside yourself when others disagree with you, a serious self-examination may be the most important thing in your life.

- If you have reached a level of responsibility and authority that is meaningful, stop and think about how you are—or are not—mentoring the next generation of leaders in your organization. They aren't likely to reach out to you, so you will need to reach out to them and offer to share some of the hard lessons you've learned over the years.
- If you haven't yet reached a serious level of authority, look upward and seek out a mentor. Look for someone who demonstrates a decentered and selfless nature. It's OK to ask them directly if you can call on them for advice from time to time. Most people will be flattered if asked this question—and if they aren't, they probably wouldn't be a good mentor in any case.
- Ask yourself: What am I doing today to give back?

CHAPTER NINE

Completing Your Personal Leadership Development Plan

Now that you've learned a great deal more about Fourth Wave leadership, you should be in a position to complete your Personal Development Plan.

You've already taken a look at the things you think are important in life (Your Strategic Baseline-Chapter 3), taken a look at how the way you value (Foundation Matrix-Chapter 4), and set strategic goals (Mission & Vision-Chapter 4).

Two more things remain for you to do to have a well-developed plan for improving your leadership skills and, more importantly, the way you perform as a leader.

Both are simple exercises that will bring you full circle in the process of understanding your leadership development plan.

To start, you should confirm that your strategic goals are in balance. To do that, review your strategic goals and look at the Foundation Matrix. Then compare the goals and your view of your relationships. You should have goals that, in one way or another, reflect these five general categories:

- Mind, body & spirit
- Family
- Friends & community
- Ethics & integrity
- Career goals

If you don't see a roughly equal dispersion of strategic goals in these categories, or if you see that your goals are not consistent with any foundation matrix interactions that are negative and weak or moderate and weak, you should rethink your strategic agenda. Review your blind spots and perhaps re-read Chapter 4.

The Personal Leadership Development spreadsheet we've developed to help you track your planning and actions can help you do this. Start by developing some balance goals (Step F in the workbook, which incorporates the five areas above) and then, on the Summary Plan worksheet, you'll be able to look at the strategic goals you've already formulated and make a direct comparison to your goals for balance.

Pasick Personal Leadership Development Plan **Review of Strategic Plans** *Make sure your plans are balanced*		
Health Goals: Mind, Body, Spirit	Date Goal Was Set	Metrics For Success
Family Goals:	Date Goal Was Set	Metrics For Success
Social Goals: Friends & Community	Date Goal Was Set	Metrics For Success
Standards Goals: Ethics & Integrity	Date Goal Was Set	Metrics For Success
Specific Career Goals	Date Goal Was Set	Metrics For Success

Naturally, you are unlikely to have a perfect balance. There's likely to be something in your life or career pushing you or pulling you further in one direction and not as hard in another and the idea that all five strategic goals will neatly divide into the five balance categories isn't the most probable outcome.

When you've completed your review, you may need to revise your "Forever Goals" (Step A worksheet) and perhaps make changes.

Once you are satisfied that your strategic goals are reasonable, match acceptably with your relationships, and have satisfactory balance, you need to do one final thing that will translate all of your work up to this point into action.

First, for each strategic goal, set an objective for that goal that you want to achieve in the next year or so. Decide on when you expect to be done with that intermediate goal and choose some method (or "metric") to compare your actual outcome with your goal. This can be done easily with the Step D form in the workbook we've created.

Pasick Personal Leadership Development Plan
What Do You Need To Accomplish *In The* <u>Next Year</u> To Reach Your Strategic Goals?
These Goals Must Be Measurable—Metrics Matter!

		Date Intermediate Goal Was Set	Target Completion Date	Metrics For Success	With whose support?
Strategic Goal No. 1					
Intermediate Goal No. 1					
Strategic Goal No. 2		Date Intermediate Goal Was Set	Target Completion Date	Metrics For Success	With whose support?
Intermediate Goal No. 2					
Strategic Goal No. 3		Date Intermediate Goal Was Set	Target Completion Date	Metrics For Success	With whose support?
Intermediate Goal No. 3					
Strategic Goal No. 4		Date Intermediate Goal Was Set	Target Completion Date	Metrics For Success	With whose support?
Intermediate Goal No. 4					
Strategic Goal No. 5		Date Intermediate Goal Was Set	Target Completion Date	Metrics For Success	With whose support?
Intermediate Goal No. 5					

Then, further break down each intermediate goal into something specific you want to accomplish in the next quarter—a short term goal—again adding dates and metrics. The Step E worksheet makes this quite easy.

Pasick Personal Leadership Development Plan
What Do You Need To Accomplish *In The* <u>Next Year</u> To Reach Your Strategic Goals?
These Goals Must Be Measurable--Metrics Matter!

Strategic Goal No. 1		Date Short-Term Goal Was Set	Target Completion Date	Metrics For Success	With whose support?
Short-Term Goal No. 1					
Strategic Goal No. 2		Date Short-Term Goal Was Set	Target Completion Date	Metrics For Success	With whose support?
Short-Term Goal No. 2					
Strategic Goal No. 3		Date Short-Term Goal Was Set	Target Completion Date	Metrics For Success	With whose support?
Short-Term Goal No. 3					
Strategic Goal No. 4		Date Short-Term Goal Was Set	Target Completion Date	Metrics For Success	With whose support?
Short-Term Goal No. 4					
Strategic Goal No. 5		Date Short-Term Goal Was Set	Target Completion Date	Metrics For Success	With whose support?
Short-Term Goal No. 5					

You should be able to complete this breakdown process in short order. Once that's done, you are now in a position to devise a simple action plan for each strategic goal so that you will have a much better chance of your plan succeeding.

And, as we have throughout this planning process, we've created a simple Action Plan worksheet for each of the five short term goals you developed. You'll probably have three or four steps that you'll need to work through to reach each short-term goal. The forms will help you do that.

To use this workbook in the future, review your action plans regularly. Modify them (and your short-term plans) as you work through the tasks on your action plans. At the end of the quarter, revise your short-term goals to achieve the next elements of each yearly intermediate goal, and update the action plans accordingly.

Last but not least, return to your strategic goals and leadership baseline once a year and modify your plan to continue your development.

Some of you may look at all of this "writing it down" as too much effort. But we ask you to trust us—we've both applied this approach ourselves and have also used it as a tool to help others develop their leadership potential.

At most, the entire process takes less than two hours for nearly everyone, and it's a mind-stretching exercise that we know will help you understand yourself in a way that you haven't before.

Writing down your plan matters because good writing leads to good thinking. More importantly, in the remote work world, which is going to be dramatically more significant (Work 4.0 perhaps?) as a result of COVID-19, good leaders and proficient managers will be forced to rely much more heavily on written communication—transmitted and managed electronically—but written, nonetheless. You simply won't be able to just carry ideas in your head and be an effective leader; that very notion may seem like something from the Dark Ages in ten years.

And self-understanding, matched with the clear thinking required to write, is a cornerstone nearly every successful technical leader will lay in careers of the future.

Sources & More Reading
Preface

Robert Pasick with Kathleen O'Gorman, "Balanced Leadership in Unbalanced Times," Front Edge Publishing LLC, January 2009.

Devon McGinnis, "What is the Fourth Industrial Revolution?", December 2018 (https://www.salesforce.com/blog/2018/12/what-is-the-fourth-industrial-revolution-4IR.html)

Introduction

Sun Tzu, "The Art of War," dated 5th century B.C. is widely available on-line as a free download.

Niccolò Machiavelli, "The Prince," 1532, is widely available on-line as a free download.

Ralph Stogdill, "Handbook of Leadership: A Survey of Theory and Research," Free Press, 1975. Many different editions, including those edited and annotated by Bernard M. Bass, are available.

James MacGregor Burns, "Leadership," Harper Collins, 1978

Larry Bossidy, "What Your Leader Expects of You," Harvard Business Review, April 2007

Chapter One

Paramount Pictures "Star Trek" series, Season 1, Episode 28. First aired 3/30/1967

Bureau of Justice:
https://www.bjs.gov/index.cfm?ty=tp&tid=311

The original story of Robert Kearns appeared in *The New Yorker:* John Seabrook, , "Flash of Genius," January 1993 (https://www.newyorker.com/magazine/1993/01/11/the-flash-of-genius)

Chapter Two

"Worlds of Robert A. Heinlein," Ace Books, 1966

Regis McKenna, "The Regis Touch," Basic Books, January 1986

Alan Lakein, "How to Get Control of Your Time and Life," Signet, February 1989

Maria Edgeworth, "Harry and Lucy Concluded," 1825- public domain

Takahashi, Kato, Matsuura, Mobbs, Suhara, Okubo, "When Your Gain Is My Pain and Your Pain Is My Gain: Neural Correlates of Envy and Schadenfreude," *Science,* 13 Feb 2009; Vol. 323, Issue 5916

Chapter Three

Jennifer Delgado, "The 12 Irrational Beliefs of Albert Ellis That Can Ruin Your Life," (https://psychology-spot.com/irrational-beliefs-albert-ellis/)

Chapter Four

The French role in the American Revolutionary War is well documented in *Wikipedia*

(https://en.wikipedia.org/wiki/France_in_the_American_Revolutionary_War)

Chapter Five

Robert Fritz, "The Path of Least Resistance for Managers Second Edition," Newfane Press, January 2011

Harvey Seifter and Peter Economy, "Leadership Ensemble: Lessons in Collaborative Management from the World's Only Conductorless Orchestra," Times Books, 2001.

Mark McNamara, "The Orpheus Effect Revisited," San Francisco Classical Voice, March 2018. (https://www.sfcv.org/article/the-orpheus-effect-revisited)

David L. Strayer and Frank A. Drews, "Profiles in Driver Distraction: Effects of Cell Phone Conversations on Younger and Older Drivers," Journal of Human Factors, December 2004

Theodore Roosevelt, "Citizenship in a Republic," a speech delivered at The Sorbonne in Paris, April 1910

Chapter Six

Alfred P. Sloane, "My Years with General Motors," Doubleday, 1963

John A. Byrne, "Chainsaw: The Notorious Career of Al Dunlap in the Era of Profit-at-Any-Price," Harper Business, 2003

Institute for Mental Health Initiatives, "Learning to Manage Anger: Discussion Leader's Manual for the Rethink Workout for Teens," Research Press, 1988

Andrew S. Grove, "Only the Paranoid Survive: How to Exploit the Crisis Points That Challenge Every Company," Currency, March 1999

Lee Berk, Stanley Tan, David Nieman, and William Eby, "Stress from Maximal Exercise Modifies T-Helper and T-Suppressor Lymphocyte Subpopulations and Their Ratio in Man," paper presented at the Annual Meeting of the American College of Sports Medicine, 1987

Rick Brenner, "Organizational Feuds" (http://www.chacocanyon.com/essays/feuds.shtml)

Chapter Seven

Jim Collins and Jerry Porras, "Built to Last: Successful Habits of Visionary Companies (Good to Great)," Harper Business, 1994

A contrary view of "Built to Last" was penned by Jennifer Reingold and Ryan Underwood in *Fast Company* in 2004 in their assessment titled, "Was "Built To Last" Built To Last?" (https://www.fastcompany.com/50992/was-built-last-built-last)

Richard Beckhard and David Richard, Organization Development: Strategies and Models, Addison-Wesley, Reading, MA, 1969

Jim Collins, "Good to Great: Why Some Companies Make the Leap and Others Don't," Harper Business, 2001

Thomas Kolditz, "In Extremis Leadership: Leading As If Your Life Depended On It," Jossey-Bass, 2007

Robert Pasick, "Awakening from the Deep Sleep : A Powerful Guide for Courageous Men," Harper San Francisco, 1993

Chapter Eight

Nic Fleming and Roger Highfield, "Contagious yawning 'shows more empathy with other people's feelings'" *The Telegraph,* September 10, 2007 (https://www.fastcompany.com/50992/was-built-last-built-last)

Platek SM1, Mohamed FB, Gallup GG Jr., Brain Res Cogn Brain Res. 2005 May;23(2-3):448-52. E-pub January 26, 2005 (https://www.ncbi.nlm.nih.gov/pubmed/15820652)

Steven Covey, "The 7 Habits of Highly Effective People: Powerful Lessons in Personal Change," Free Press, November 2004

Tom Rath and Donald O. Clifton, "How Full Is Your Bucket?" Gallup Press, August 2004

Jean M. Twenge, "Generation Me: Why Today's Young Americans Are More Confident, Assertive, Entitled--and More Miserable Than Ever Before," Free Press, April 2006

Jean M. Twenge, Stacy M. Campbell, Journal of Managerial Psychology, 2008, Volume 23, Issue 8

Richard Sheridan, "Chief Joy Officer: How Great Leaders Elevate Human Energy and Eliminate Fear," Portfolio Books, 2018

Keith H. Hammonds, "Why We Hate HR," *Fast Company,* August 1, 2005 (https://www.fastcompany.com/53319/why-we-hate-hr)

Mike Wilson, "The Difference between God and Larry Ellison: God Doesn't Think He's Larry Ellison," HarperCollins 2003

Made in the USA
Monee, IL
27 June 2020